# R2DBC Revealed

## Reactive Relational Database Connectivity for Java and JVM Programmers

**Robert Hedgpeth**

*Foreword by Mark Paluch, R2DBC Spec Lead*

Apress®

*R2DBC Revealed: Reactive Relational Database Connectivity for Java and JVM Programmers*

Robert Hedgpeth
Chicago, IL, USA

ISBN-13 (pbk): 978-1-4842-6988-6
https://doi.org/10.1007/978-1-4842-6989-3

ISBN-13 (electronic): 978-1-4842-6989-3

Managing Director, Apress Media LLC: Welmoed Spahr
Acquisitions Editor: Jonathan Gennick
Development Editor: Laura Berendson
Coordinating Editor: Jill Balzano

Cover image designed by Freepik (www.freepik.com)

Distributed to the book trade worldwide by Springer Science+Business Media LLC, 1 New York Plaza, Suite 4600, New York, NY 10004. Phone 1-800-SPRINGER, fax (201) 348-4505, e-mail orders-ny@springer-sbm. com, or visit www.springeronline.com. Apress Media, LLC is a California LLC and the sole member (owner) is Springer Science + Business Media Finance Inc (SSBM Finance Inc). SSBM Finance Inc is a **Delaware** corporation.

For information on translations, please e-mail booktranslations@springernature.com; for reprint, paperback, or audio rights, please e-mail bookpermissions@springernature.com.

Apress titles may be purchased in bulk for academic, corporate, or promotional use. eBook versions and licenses are also available for most titles. For more information, reference our Print and eBook Bulk Sales web page at http://www.apress.com/bulk-sales.

Any source code or other supplementary material referenced by the author in this book is available to readers on GitHub via the book's product page, located at www.apress.com/9781484269886. For more detailed information, please visit http://www.apress.com/source-code.

Printed on acid-free paper

*To my beautiful, intelligent, and incredibly patient wife, Tracy, for encouraging and supporting me throughout all the nights and weekends I spent on this book, and to our infant son, Darius, for providing ample opportunities for early morning writing.*

# Table of Contents

# About the Author

**Robert Hedgpeth** is a professional software engineer, speaker, and developer relations enthusiast residing in the bustling metropolis of Chicago, Illinois. Rob has more than 15 years of professional development experience, primarily in the application development space. Throughout the years, he has contributed to the architecture and development of many solutions, using a large array of languages and technologies. Now, as a developer advocate and evangelist, Rob gets to combine his love for technology with his mission to fuel developers' curiosity and passion. Follow him on Twitter: @probablyrealrob.

# About the Technical Reviewer

 **Brian Molt** is a software developer at a manufacturing company in Nebraska where he has been for 17 years. During his time there, he has programmed with multiple languages on a variety of platforms, including RPGLE on an AS/400, web development with ASP.NET, and desktop application development with JavaFX, and now he creates REST services using JAX-RS.

# Acknowledgments

I'm not going to lie. Writing my first book has been an incredibly daunting and challenging task. I spent many long nights, early mornings, and weekends researching, writing, researching some more, and rewriting. But absolutely none of it would have been possible without the help from some amazing people.

First, I'd like to thank the Apress team, as this book wouldn't have been possible without the opportunity provided by Jonathan Gennick, Jill Balzano, Laura Berendson, and the rest of the amazing folks at Apress. A special thank you, Brian Molt, for not only providing technical expertise but also the insight of a teammate who was truly invested in the success of this book.

Next, I'd like to thank Mark Paluch, the spec lead for the R2DBC specification. You were incredibly helpful and encouraging throughout the whole process and provided extremely thorough feedback for all of my questions.

And last, and most importantly, I'd like to thank my wonderful wife, Tracy. Writing a book isn't easy. Writing a book during a global pandemic and as first-time parents is a whole other level. Absolutely none of this would have been possible without your support, encouragement, and patience.

# The World at Scale

A Foreword by Mark Paluch

One of the few stable things in information technology is constant change.

Software, once written as machine code, then by using compilers, went (and still goes) through various paradigm changes: procedural, data driven, object oriented, functional. There have been many more programming models, and others will follow. Patterns come and go as we speak. All this is driven by purpose, capabilities of our runtime environments, constraints, and business requirements.

In a similar way, the way how we consume software services has changed many times. Back in the 1990s, software was primarily installed locally and sometimes backed by a server. Think of your good old desktop computer. The 2000s are characterized by online services. More and more services became available through the Internet, all hosted in their own data centers. Businesses began investigating web applications to avoid installing software on each machine. Data centers grew.

The 2010s finally set the stage for software-backed services to run in the cloud. Many online services were founded these years. It's the golden digital age. Businesses driven by software can simply scale by adding another batch of machines to their data center to serve more customers, or in their cloud.

Scalability is only constrained by the remaining capacity in a data center, the investment in servers, and the operational cost for computer systems. Scaling a business comes with many challenges. One of them is efficiency. Efficiency becomes an important metric to measure how well a system is utilized compared to its cost.

But what impacts the efficiency and scalability of an application?

To answer this question, we have to get to the bottom of an application and its programming language. Are you ready to dig through the physiology of applications? Ready? Go!

All applications have in common that they require computation power and memory to fulfill their work. How many concurrent requests/users/processes/<insert your measurement unit here> a single machine can handle depends primarily on CPU and memory demand. It also depends on "how" CPU and memory are used with a strong tie to the duration in which resources get occupied.

Typical enterprise applications on the JVM follow an imperative programming style that guarantees synchronization and order of execution for each individual statement.

Imperative programming comes with certain effects that aren't immediately visible. One of these effects is how I/O gets handled and how it affects threads. Typically, applications require an integration with a database, message broker, or another remote service to perform their work. When communicating with remote integrations, the network becomes an integral part of the work that has to be done. It becomes a driver for latency. Network performance and remote peer performance become a factor that affects scalability as I/O causes to block the underlying thread. Threads require memory and CPU. You can't have an infinite number. That being said, threads impose a primary constraint for application scalability.

With sufficiently high I/O load, machines can be kept busy with waiting for I/O – they basically wait all the time with CPU and memory being maxed out. As you might already tell, such an arrangement isn't efficient.

Now that we have identified constraints for scalability and efficiency, we should take a look at what we can do about this aspect.

There are various approaches to overcome the limitations of the imperative programming model. The most significant and most efficient one is just not using blocking I/O. Using non-blocking I/O is all but trivial.

In the JVM space, we can use various abstractions that help with developing highly efficient applications. So far, the only consistent programming model that helps with non-blocking I/O is reactive programming. Reactive programming is heavily stream and event oriented. It is characterized by pipeline definitions, operators, and a functional programming style. Reactive programming leads to a well-structured code that isn't cluttered with endless callbacks.

Data sources, internal and inter-process sources, follow the same style. The reactive runtime and its integrations encapsulate threading and the non-blocking I/O business. Reactive drivers expose a convenient API that can be directly used without worrying about how to use non-blocking I/O.

Reactive programming on the JVM is still a young endeavor. In the past years, an inter-op standard emerged to connect reactive libraries so that they can interact with each other. This standard is Reactive Streams.

The very first abstractions that followed Reactive Streams were composition libraries, web frameworks, messaging libraries, and the MongoDB client.

Over time, the number of reactive database clients grew, but all of these were targeting NoSQL data stores: MongoDB, Redis, Cassandra, and Couchbase. However, large parts of data are still hosted in SQL databases.

The standard way to access SQL databases on the JVM is JDBC. JDBC uses a blocking API model which renders JDBC unusable for reactive programming.

The growing adoption of reactive programming raised continuously the question of how to integrate with SQL databases in general and how to use existing libraries to run queries and map objects in particular. Using JDBC on a ThreadPool may help for small-scale applications. ThreadPools however do not turn blocking behavior into non-blocking – the blocking problem is just put somewhere else instead of solving it.

Facing demand from reactive application developers, without an existing standardized API, a small group of developers formed to investigate how reactive applications could be integrated with SQL databases. And that was the inception of R2DBC in 2017, an open standard to let the world run at scale using reactive programming with SQL databases.

Mark Paluch
R2DBC Spec Lead
March 2021

# Introduction

I think it goes without saying that software users' expectations have never been higher. With the standards of performance and usability continually rising, we developers have been challenged to innovate like never before. Reactive programming has provided us an avenue toward such innovation.

However, for far too long, we weren't able to achieve fully reactive solutions within the Java ecosystem. We've been limited to trying to work around the blocking nature of the Java Database Connectivity (JDBC) Application Programming Interface (API) within our reactive solutions. But along came the Reactive Relational Database Connectivity (R2DBC) specification, and suddenly the doors to developing fully reactive applications flung open.

Starting by gaining a solid understanding of reactive programming and what it means to use declarative programming techniques, we'll lay the foundation for not only what it is and how it works but *why* it's so important.

Diving into the specification, you'll learn how a relatively small collection of interfaces and classes makes it possible to create a lightweight driver implementation that, utilizing the power of the Reactive Streams API, completely unblocks your applications' interactions to underlying relational data storage solutions.

So, whether you've been creating reactive applications for years or at this very moment are like "What the heck is reactive programming?", my hope is that by the time you've finished this book, you will have not only a solid understanding of the R2DBC specification but also the confidence, provided in part by practical solution code and samples, to start creating your own solutions using R2DBC.

# PART I

# The Reactive Movement and R2DBC

# CHAPTER 1

# The Case for Reactive Programming

Buzzword technologies are all too familiar within the software engineering world. For years, some of the most creative minds have given us development innovations that have completely changed the landscape of our solutions. On the other hand, some of those trending technologies have caused us much more pain in the long run. All the hype can be difficult to assess.

In this first chapter, I'd like to address the paradigm of *reactive programming*, which has been gaining popularity for several years, and help to lay the groundwork for our journey into the idea of Reactive Relational Database Connectivity (R2DBC).

Since you're reading this book, I'm going to assume that you have likely at least heard or read the words "reactive" and "programming" paired together before this point. Heck, I'll even go out on a limb and guess that you might have even heard or read that in order to create a truly reactive solution, you need to think reactively. But what does all of that even mean? Well, let's find out!

## A Traditional Approach

Introducing new technologies can be challenging, but I've found that it can help to identify a common, real-world use case that we, as developers, have encountered and see how it fits within that context.

Imagine a basic solution that contains web request workflow between a client application and a server application, and let's start at the point where there's an asynchronous request initiated from the client to the server.

© Robert Hedgpeth 2021
R. Hedgpeth, *R2DBC Revealed*, https://doi.org/10.1007/978-1-4842-6989-3_1

**Note**   When something is occurring *asynchronously*, it means that there is a relationship between two or more events/objects that interact within the same system but don't occur at predetermined intervals and don't necessarily rely on each other's existence to function. Put more simply, they are events that are not coordinated with each other and happen simultaneously.

Upon receiving the request, the server spins up a new thread for processing (Figure 1-1).

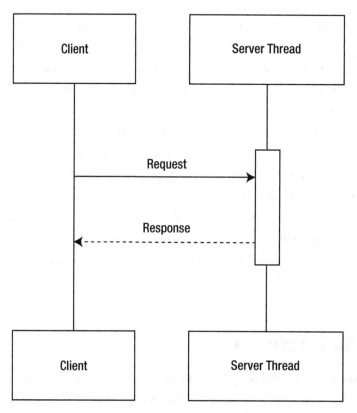

***Figure 1-1.*** *Executing a simple, synchronous web request from a client to server*

Simple enough, and it runs, so ship it, right? Not so fast! Rarely is it the case that requests are *that* simple. It could be the case, like in Figure 1-2, that the server thread needs to access a database to complete the work requested by the client. However, while the database is being accessed, the server thread waits, blocking more work from being performed until a response is returned by the database.

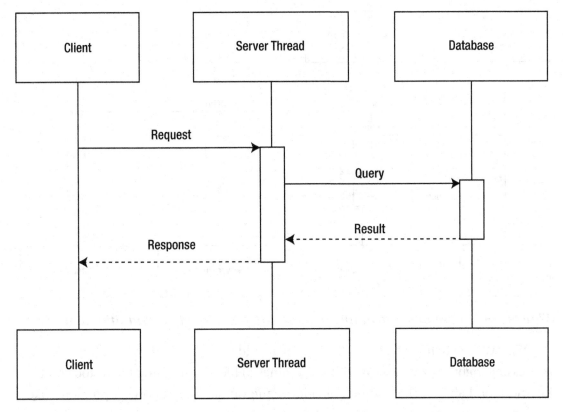

***Figure 1-2.*** *The server thread is blocked from performing work while the database returns a response*

Unfortunately, that's probably not an optimal solution as there's no way to know how long the database call will take. That's not likely to scale well. So, in an effort to optimize the client's time and keep it working, you could add more threads to process multiple requests in parallel, like in Figure 1-3.

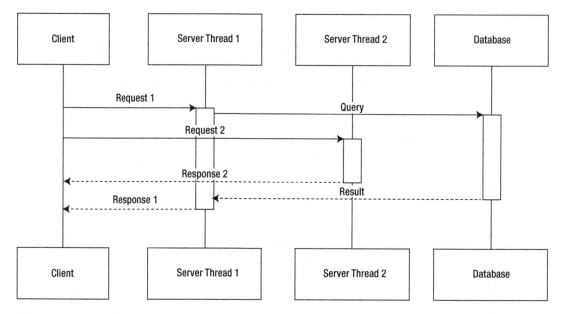

**Figure 1-3.** *Subsequent incoming requests are processed using additional threads*

Now we're cooking! You can just continue to add threads to handle additional processing, right? Not so fast. As with most things in life, if something seems too good to be true, it probably is. The trade-off for adding additional threads is pesky problems like higher resource consumption, possibly resulting in decreased throughput, and, in many cases, increased complexity for developers due to thread context management.

---

**Note**    For many applications, using multiple threads will work as a viable solution. Reactive programming is not a silver bullet. However, reactive solutions can help utilize resources more efficiently. Read on to learn how!

---

# Imperative vs. Declarative Programming

Using multiple threads to prevent blocking operations is a common approach within *imperative* programming paradigms and languages. That's because the imperative approach is a process that describes, step-by-step, the state a program should be in to accomplish a specific goal. Ultimately, imperative processes hinge on controlling the flow of information, which can be very useful in certain situations, but can also create quite a headache, as I alluded to before, with memory and thread management.

*Declarative* programming, on the other hand, does not focus on how to accomplish a specific goal but rather the goal itself. But that's fairly vague, so let's back up a bit.

Consider the following analogies:

- **Imperative programming** is like attending an art class and listening to the teacher give you step-by-step instructions on how to paint a landscape.

- **Declarative programming** is like attending an art class and being told to paint a landscape. The teacher doesn't care how you do it, just that it gets done.

---

**Tip**    Both imperative and declarative programming paradigms have strengths and weaknesses. Like with any task, make sure you choose the right tool for the job!

---

For this book, I'm going to be using the Java programming languages for all the examples. Now, it's no secret that Java is an imperative language, and as such its focus is on how to achieve the final result. That said, it's easy for us to imagine how to write imperative instructions using Java, but what you may not know is that you can also write declarative flows. For instance, consider the following.

Here's an imperative approach to summing a range of numbers, step-by-step, from one to ten:

```
int sum = 0;
for (int i = 1; i <= 10; i++) {
    sum += i;
}
System.out.println(sum); // 55
```

Alternatively, a declarative approach to summing a range of numbers from one to ten involves working with data streams and receiving a result as some unknown, or rather unspecified, time in the future:

```
int sumByStream = IntStream.rangeClosed(0,10).sum();
System.out.println(sumByStream); // 55
```

---

**Note**    In Java 8, streams were introduced as part of an effort to increase
the declarative programming capabilities within the language. `IntStream`
`rangeClosed(int startInclusive, int endInclusive)` returns an
`IntStream` from `startInclusive` (inclusive) to `endInclusive` (inclusive) by
an incremental step of 1.

---

However, for the time being, it's not important that you understand a `Stream` object
or the underlying `IntStream` specialization. No, for now, set the idea of a "stream" to the
side; we'll get back to it.

The real takeaway here is that both approaches yield the same results, but the
declarative approach is merely setting an expectation for the result of an operation, not
dictating the underlying implementation steps. This is fundamentally, from a high level,
how *reactive programming* works. Still a little hazy? Let's dive deeper.

# Thinking Reactively

As I mentioned previously, reactive programming, at its core, is declarative. It aims
to circumvent blocking states by eliminating many of the issues caused by having to
maintain numerous threads. Ultimately, this is accomplished by managing expectations
between the client and server.

In fact, pursuing a more *reactive* approach, upon receiving a request from the client,
the server thread calls on the database for processing, but does not wait for a response.
This frees up the server thread to continue processing incoming requests. Then, at an
undetermined amount of time later, a response, in the form of an event, is received and
reacted to by the server thread from the database.

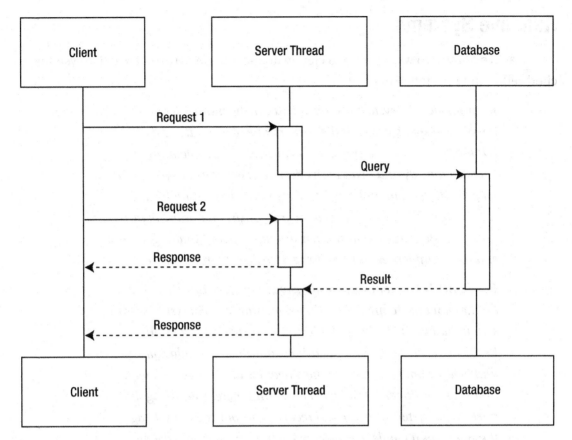

**Figure 1-4.** *The client does not wait for a direct response from the server*

The non-blocking and event-driven behaviors displayed in Figure 1-4 are the foundation which reactive programming is built on.

# The Reactive Manifesto

I know what you're thinking. The overall concept behind reactive programming isn't new, so why the hype? Well, it started with the formalization of what constitutes a reactive system.

In 2013, the Reactive Manifesto was created as a way to address new requirements, at the time, in application development and provide a common vocabulary for discussing complex concepts, like reactive programming. And then, in 2014, it was revised, via version 2.0, to more accurately reflect the core value of reactive design.

# Reactive Systems

The Reactive Manifesto was created to clearly define four objectives of reactive systems, cited verbatim in the following:

> ***Responsive:*** *The system responds in a timely manner if at all possible. Responsiveness is the cornerstone of usability and utility, but more than that, responsiveness means that problems may be detected quickly and dealt with effectively. Responsive systems focus on providing rapid and consistent response times, establishing reliable upper bounds so they deliver a consistent quality of service. This consistent behaviour in turn simplifies error handling, builds end user confidence, and encourages further interaction.*
>
> ***Resilient:*** *The system stays responsive in the face of failure. This applies not only to highly-available, mission-critical systems—any system that is not resilient will be unresponsive after a failure. Resilience is achieved by replication, containment, isolation and delegation. Failures are contained within each component, isolating components from each other and thereby ensuring that parts of the system can fail and recover without compromising the system as a whole. Recovery of each component is delegated to another (external) component and high-availability is ensured by replication where necessary. The client of a component is not burdened with handling its failures.*
>
> ***Elastic:*** *The system stays responsive under varying workload. Reactive Systems can react to changes in the input rate by increasing or decreasing the* <u>*resources*</u> *allocated to service these inputs. This implies designs that have no contention points or central bottlenecks, resulting in the ability to shard or replicate components and distribute inputs among them. Reactive Systems support predictive, as well as Reactive, scaling algorithms by providing relevant live performance measures. They achieve elasticity in a cost-effective way on commodity hardware and software platforms.*

*Message Driven: Reactive Systems rely on asynchronous message-passing to establish a boundary between components that ensures loose coupling, isolation and location transparency. This boundary also provides the means to delegate failures as messages. Employing explicit message-passing enables load management, elasticity, and flow control by shaping and monitoring the message queues in the system and applying back-pressure when necessary. Location transparent messaging as a means of communication makes it possible for the management of failure to work with the same constructs and semantics across a cluster or within a single host. Non-blocking communication allows recipients to only consume resources while active, leading to less system overhead.*

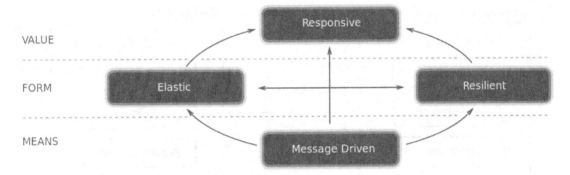

***Figure 1-5.***  *The four tenets of the Reactive Manifesto*

Put more simply, a reactive system is an architectural approach that seeks to combine multiple, independent solutions into a single, cohesive unit that, as a whole, remains responsive, or *reactive*, to the world around it with the solutions simultaneously remaining aware of each other. And put as simply as possible, a reactive system is when a unit, adhering to a set of guidelines, of the system remains reactive to each of the other units within the same system that, using those same guidelines, is collectively reactive to external systems.

# Reactive Systems != Reactive Programming

At this point, it would be easy to confuse the terms "reactive system" and "reactive programming" as being interchangeable, but it's important to note that the use of reactive programming within a solution does not make the solution a reactive system.

As previously mentioned, the Reactive Manifesto was revised a year after it was created, and one of the updates was to establish one of the core tenants of reactive systems to involve the usage of asynchronous *message-passing*. Reactive programming, on the other hand, is *event-driven*.

So what's the difference? Reactive systems rely on the usage of messaging to create resilient and elastic solutions for distributed systems (Figure 1-6). Typically, messages have a target destination. In contrast, events are used within a smaller, more concise scope and do not have an intended destination.

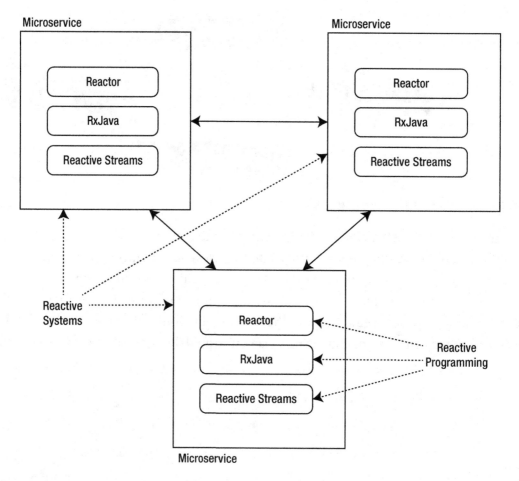

*Figure 1-6.*  *Reactive systems vs. reactive programming*

An event is a signal by one component upon reaching a certain state that can be observed by any attached listeners. Don't worry. I'll dive deeper into how events are observed by listeners in the upcoming sections.

## Asynchronous Data Streams

But working with events isn't a novel concept. In fact, user interface events, like button clicks and various other control interactions, are nothing more than asynchronous event streams that can be subscribed to, observed, and reacted to.

## Data Streams

Similarly, reactive programming uses data streams which are sequences of ongoing events, ordered in time (Figure 1-7). There are three types of events that can be observed from a data stream: a value, an error, and a completion signal.

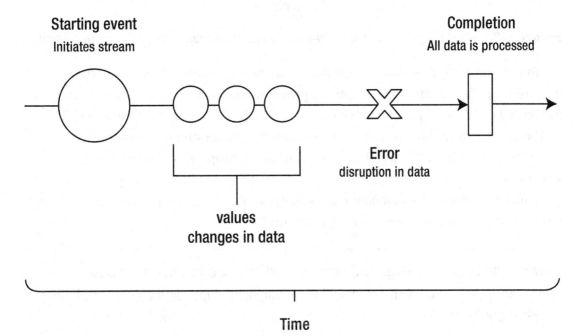

*Figure 1-7.* *The anatomy of a data stream*

Emitted events within the stream are observed asynchronously, or at intermittent intervals, which allows data stream subscribers to respond in turn, or *reactively* (Figure 1-8).

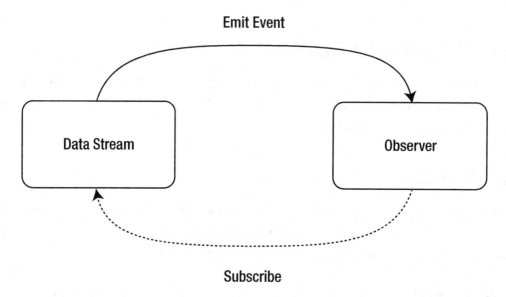

**Figure 1-8.** *Subscribing observers respond to emitted events from the data stream*

At this point, it's important to note that data streams are not limited to sending only user interface events. In fact, reactive programming as a whole wouldn't be very interesting or so broadly useful if that were the case. So, just as the name suggests, if it's data, which most things are, it can be streamed in a data stream. This includes, but is certainly not limited to, variables, user input values, properties, objects, and data structures.

If this all seems somewhat familiar, it's likely because you, at some point in your life, have learned about the Observer Design Pattern.

---

**Note**    The Observer Design Pattern is defined as a one-to-many relationship between objects such as if one object is modified, its dependent objects are to be notified automatically.

---

# Back Pressure

The usage of data streams, between publishers, those sending data, and subscribers is simple enough to understand. In a perfect world, the flow of data would happen at a rate where elements, items, or basically some unknown amounts of data are published and consumed at the same pace (Figure 1-9).

***Figure 1-9.***  *The ideal state of a publisher and subscriber*

However, because we don't live in a perfect world, using this approach, it's possible that data can be emitted at a higher rate than the subscriber can handle. If this happens, the subscriber will need to create a backlog of work that is pending processing (Figure 1-10).

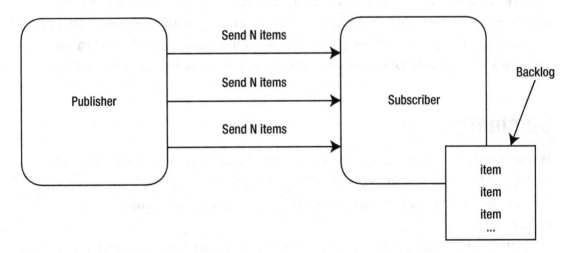

***Figure 1-10.***  *If the publisher emits elements faster than the subscriber can handle them, a backlog of unprocessed elements is created*

Luckily, the problem can be solved by simply allowing a subscriber to communicate with a publisher that it's ready to receive more elements. This feedback process is known as back pressure, and it plays a crucial part in facilitating effective reactive solutions. However, it's not as simple as just allowing the subscriber to communicate directly with the publisher, which could simply offload the problem of accumulating a backlog of work to the publisher as the publisher may not be able to publish data at the rate requested by the subscriber (Figure 1-11).

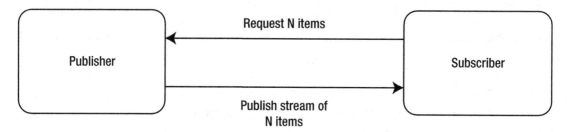

***Figure 1-11.*** *The simplest implementation of back pressure*

Using back pressure to efficiently utilize asynchronous data streams plays a pivotal role in facilitating efficient reactive programming solutions. However, it's also not a trivial problem to solve, but, luckily, there are a variety of methods through which back pressure can be implemented. In the next chapter, I'll explore a specification called Reactive Streams that R2DBC uses to create truly reactive database communication.

# Summary

In this chapter, you received an overview of what reactive programming is, when it's useful, and how it works. You've gained a high-level understanding of how declarative programming helps facilitate asynchronous data streams to create non-blocking, reactive solutions.

In the next chapter, we'll examine how these principles have been utilized to facilitate reactive interactions with relational databases using Reactive Relational Database Connectivity (R2DBC).

# CHAPTER 2

# Introduction to R2DBC

It should come as no surprise that reactive programming has been a game change for application development. As I explained in the previous chapter, it can be extremely useful in creating non-blocking solutions that help to optimize resource usage. But in order for a solution to be truly reactive, it must be so *pervasively*, including database interactions.

After all, a large majority of applications require some kind of persistence storage, and many use relational databases to fill that role. Relational databases have existed for decades, and as such many of the technologies, like the Java Database Connectivity (JDBC) Application Programming Interface (API), used to connect to and communicate with them have also existed for many years. Because of this, having been created in a time before the rising popularity of reactive solutions, the JDBC API uses blocking operations when communicating with databases.

However, as I've previously pointed out, in order for a solution to be *truly* reactive, it needs to be so pervasively, even when dealing with databases. The increasing use of reactive programming combined with a majority of applications using relational databases prompted the industry to take a look at a solution for creating reactive interactions with relational databases.

## What Is R2DBC?

Reactive Relational Database Connectivity (R2DBC) was created to bridge the gap between relational data stores and systems using reactive programming models.

17

# A New Approach

Functionally, through the use of R2DBC, applications written in a Java Virtual Machine (JVM) programming language can run Structured Query Language (SQL) statements and retrieve results from a targeted data source, all reactively.

This is possible because R2DBC is a new, open specification that provides fully reactive programming APIs to connect to and communicate with relational data stores (Figure 2-1).

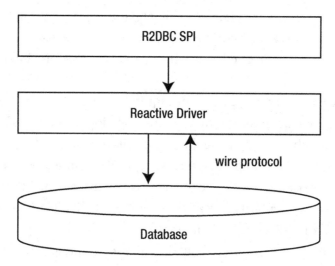

***Figure 2-1.*** *The R2DBC hierarchy and workflow*

---

**Note**    A *wire protocol* refers to a way of getting data from one point to another, a means for interoperation of one or more applications in a network. It generally refers to protocols higher than the physical layer.

---

Ultimately, by using the fundamental concepts of the reactive programming paradigm, R2DBC eliminates the blocking nature of its relational database connectivity predecessors, like JDBC (Figure 2-2).

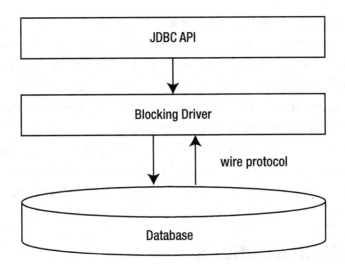

***Figure 2-2.***  *The JDBC hierarchy and workflow*

# Beyond JDBC

But why a completely new approach? You might be wondering, "Couldn't something be done to modify the JDBC API to work reactively?" The answer to that is "yes." Certainly it's possible, but at what cost?

The decision to create a new approach dates back to 2017 when the creators of R2DBC, before R2DBC existed, aspired to use an Oracle-born solution for reactively working with relational databases known as Asynchronous Database Access (ADBA), otherwise known as "java.sql2." Ideally, the group wanted to investigate a fully reactive API without having the burden of dealing with standards bodies. However, the usage of ADBA was short-lived as, upon investigation of the approach, the group failed to convince the Oracle team to incorporate certain nonnegotiable architectural changes.

---

**Note**    On September 18, 2017, at the Oracle CodeOne developer conference, Oracle announced that they would stop work on ADBA (Asynchronous Database Access).

---

Given their experiences with ADBA, the group could not convince themselves that evolving JDBC was the correct approach, instead preferring a modern and truly reactive API. Combined with the benefits of fast innovation cycles and creating an open standard, developing R2DBC as a standalone specification made the most sense. The creation of a new specification also allowed room for implementers to have more freedom on the technical direction and the dependencies therein.

Also, as previously mentioned, while R2DBC's primary focus is relational databases, it is not limited to them. Instead, the intention is to keep the focus on storage mechanisms that use SQL or a SQL-like dialect to represent data in a tabular format.

## R2DBC Implementations

R2DBC works by providing a service-provider interface (SPI). The SPI is simply a collection of interfaces that serve as a guide for relational data storage vendor implementations by defining foundational elements used to work with relational databases reactively (Figure 2-3).

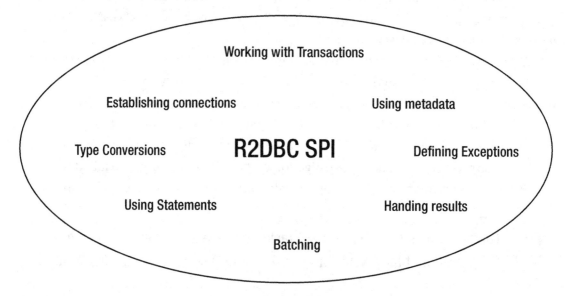

*Figure 2-3.* *Some of the capabilities defined by the R2DBC SPI*

In the next several chapters, I'll look closer into the specific interfaces that are available within the SPI and how they come together to make relational database interactions truly reactive.

Client libraries and applications can use R2DBC driver implementations, which utilize the SPI, to create fully reactive solutions (Figure 2-4).

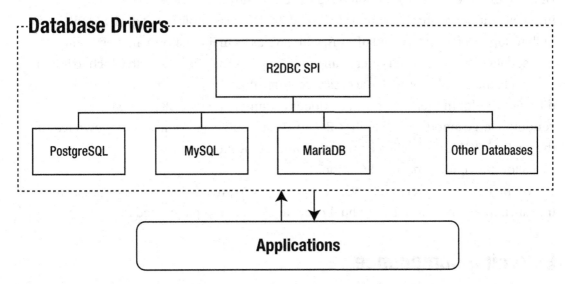

***Figure 2-4.*** *R2DBC driver implementation topology and workflow*

# Embracing Reactive Programming

Above all else, the goal of the R2DBC specification is to provide an API capable of facilitating integration with relational data stores using a reactive programming model. To achieve that goal, the specification embraces crucial properties of reactive programming that focus on efficiently utilizing resources, including the following:

- Non-blocking I/O through deferred and asynchronous execution

- Using back pressure to allow flow control, deferring the actual execution and not overwhelming consumers

- Treating application control as a series of events (data, errors, completions) and stream-oriented data consumption

- No longer assuming control of resources but leaving resource scheduling to the runtime or platform

# Enabling Vendor Creativity

Unlike JDBC, the R2DBC API is intended to be as lightweight as possible allowing implementations a large amount of flexibility. To help accomplish that goal, R2DBC was built to support reactive JVM platforms, with Java as its main platform, in their ability to access data using Structured Query Language (SQL) as the interface with which to interact.

While the SPI also provides access to features that are commonly found across many different vendor implementations, the focus on simplicity for R2DBC is what allows vendors a large amount of flexibility. Because each database comes with its own features, the goal of R2DBC is to define a minimal standard over commonly used functionality and allow for vendor-specific deviation.

Ultimately, the power of R2DBC lies in its ability to provide balance between features that are implemented in a driver and those that are better implemented in a client library.

# Enforcing Compliance

R2DBC driver implementations must fulfill a variety of requirements and pass a series of tests in order to be recognized as officially compliant. As I mentioned before, R2DBC's primary focus is on the usage of SQL with relational data stores; that's just the tip of the iceberg.

Among the many implementation requirements, the SPI must implement a non-blocking I/O layer.

---

**Stay Tuned**    In Chapter 3, I will go into more detail about the compliance requirements for R2DBC.

---

In the next section, you'll get a better understanding of how the *Reactive Streams* API allows non-blocking back pressure–aware data access.

# Reactive Streams

Previously, I introduced the concept of reactive programming and the use of back pressure to help regulate the flow of data with the help of asynchronous data streams. Recall that the concept of back pressure revolves around limiting the amount of data that's transmitted between the stages of a delivery pipeline, so that no stage in the data movement process gets overwhelmed.

*Reactive Streams* is an initiative that provides a standard, defined through a number of interfaces, used to manage asynchronous stream processing with non-blocking back pressure.

## Another Specification

Above all else, it's important to know that Reactive Streams standardizes the use of asynchronous data streams in a way that ensures the receiving side is not forced to buffer, or backlog, arbitrary amounts of data. In fact, the key objective is to mandate usage of back pressure signals in an asynchronous manner to ensure fully asynchronous, non-blocking behavior of Reactive Streams implementations.

Reactive Streams is merely a specification, and as such, the intention is to enable the creation of conforming implementations. That means that the various options of stream manipulations, such as transformation, splitting, and merging, are not handled by the specification itself. Instead, Reactive Streams is only concerned with moderating the stream of data, or the workflow, between underlying API components.

Similar to the R2DBC SPI, which I'll examine in more detail in the next chapter, the Reactive Streams specification provides a standard test suite, Technology Compatibility Kit (TCK), for testing implementation compliance. While implementations are free to implement additional features by the specification, they must conform to all Reactive Streams API requirements and pass all tests within the TCK.

## API Fundamentals

The API consists of the following components that are required to be provided by Reactive Streams implementations:

1. Publisher

2. Subscriber

3. Subscription

4. Processor

A subscriber's role is to let the publisher know that it is ready to accept a number of items, and if items are available, the publisher pushes as many items as it can, up to the maximum requested (Figure 2-5).

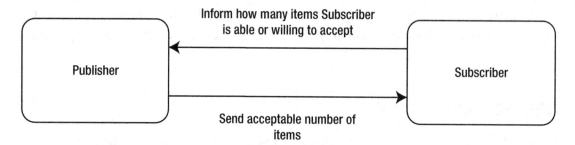

***Figure 2-5.*** *A subscriber requests items from a publisher*

This should look familiar, because as I described in the last chapter (Figure 1-11), the process of restricting the number of items that a subscriber is willing to accept is, as indicated by the subscriber itself, known as *back pressure*.

The Reactive Streams API establishes the two-way connection between a subscriber and a publisher as a subscription. Subscriptions represent a one-to-one lifecycle of a subscriber subscribing to a publisher (Figure 2-6).

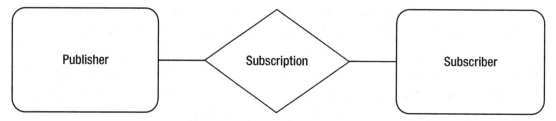

***Figure 2-6.*** *A subscription between a publisher and subscriber*

While a publisher can have many subscribers, a subscriber can only subscribe to one publisher (Figure 2-7).

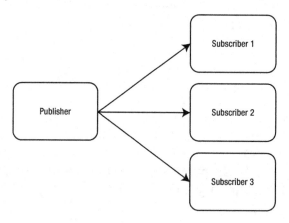

***Figure 2-7.*** *A publisher can have multiple subscribers*

After a subscriber has subscribed to a publisher, the publisher then notifies the subscriber of the subscription that's been created. Then the subscriber is free to request *n* number of items.

Once the publisher has items available, it's able to send at most *n* number of items to the subscriber. If, at any point, an error occurs within the publisher, it signals an *error*. When the publisher is finished sending data, it signals the subscriber that it is *complete*.

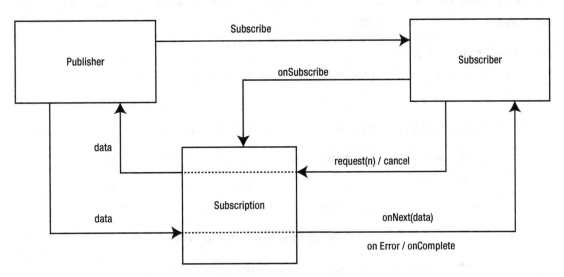

***Figure 2-8.***  *The Reactive Streams subscription workflow*

## Processors

Entities existing as both a publisher and subscriber are known as *processors*. Processors are often used as intermediaries between publishers and subscribers to handle transformations, like data filtering, on streams of data (Figure 2-9).

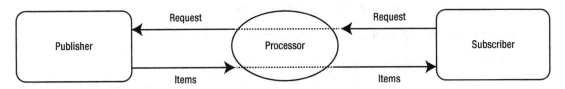

***Figure 2-9.***  *A processor being used between a publisher and subscriber*

# JVM Interfaces

As described in the previous section, Reactive Streams is made up of four main entities, *publisher, subscriber, subscription,* and *processor,* which exist as interfaces that are used to create implementation libraries within the JVM.

The *Publisher* interface only allows subscribers to subscribe to publishers through a publicly exposed method called `subscribe`. A generic type T is used to represent the type of items that the publisher produces:

```
public interface Publisher<T> {
    public void subscribe(Subscriber<? super T> s);
}
```

The *Subscriber* interface requires four methods of interaction:

1.  `onSubscribe`: Used to notify the *subscriber* of a successful subscription

2.  `onNext`: Accepts pushed items from the *publisher*

3.  `onError`: Accepts error notifications from the *publisher*

4.  `onComplete`: Accepts completion signal from the *publisher*

```
public interface Subscriber<T> {
    public void onSubscribe(Subscription s);
    public void onNext(T t);
    public void onError(Throwable t);
    public void onComplete();
}
```

*Subscription* requires two methods of interaction:

1.  `request`: Accepts requests for items from the *subscriber*

2.  `cancel`: Accepts cancellation from the *subscriber*

```
public interface Subscription {
    public void request(long n);
    public void cancel();
}
```

*Processor* is both a subscriber and publisher. A processor can produce items of a different type than the type of items that it consumes, and, because of this, generics (T, R) are used to represent the consumed and produced types:

```
public interface Processor<T, R> extends Subscriber<T>, Publisher<R> {
}
```

## Implementations

As you can imagine, there have been a variety of Reactive Streams implementations created that are available as third-party libraries that can be included within JVM applications. In fact, because of the overwhelming popularity of the Reactive Streams standard and its use within many Java packages at the time, as part of concurrency updates, the specification was added as an enhancement to the Java standard libraries as part of the Java Developer Kit (JDK) 9 release.

The inclusion of the Reactive Streams standard helped to reduce the duplication and inherent compatibility issues caused by all the usages, separated only by their package names. Since the release of Java 9, the basic Reactive Streams interfaces were included within the Flow Concurrency library, allowing Java applications to rely on a single library for Reactive Streams interfaces, rather than deciding on a specific implementation.

However, it's important to note that while the *Flow Concurrency* library is available within the JDK, the R2DBC specification uses the Reactive Streams specification *directly from source*. For instance, this means the R2DBC specification uses *Publisher* directly from `org.reactivestreams.Publisher` instead of the interface available in `java.util.concurrent.Flow`.

## Summary

In this chapter, I introduced you to Reactive Relational Database Connectivity (R2DBC), the reasons it was created, the problems it aims to solve, and how it uses the Reactive Streams API to accomplish it all.

Also, I briefly described the need for implementations to adhere to a strict level of compliance to be considered a legitimate R2DBC client. In the next chapter, I'm going to take a closer look at the SPI interfaces, how driver implementations are created using those interfaces, and the requirements of implementations to achieve full compliance with the R2DBC standard.

# PART II

# The R2DBC
# Service-Provider Interface

# CHAPTER 3

# The Path to Implementation

So far, you've learned that the R2DBC specification exists to provide a way to achieve asynchronous, non-blocking interactions with relational data stores. Going forward, I'll be specifically looking at relational database solutions and how the specification has been designed to provide the flexibility for implementations to target a variety of relational databases with very diverse types of functionality.

In an effort to provide the most versatile solution for developers, the specification aims to strike a balance of being able to support the common capabilities shared among all relational databases while also allowing the ability to highlight distinct features of specific implementations.

## The Database Landscape

As I explained in the last chapter, R2DBC, at the highest level, seeks to provide an asynchronous, non-blocking approach to querying and managing data for

1) Relational databases that use the Structured Query Language (SQL)

2) Applications written in Java Virtual Machine (JVM) programming language

If you've worked with multiple relational database solutions before, you've likely noticed that there are certain commonalities and characteristics among them, for instance, the requirement to establish a connection before being able to execute queries. Obviously, this is the case, but the specification, like the JDBC API, needs to create implementation requirements for it.

31

© Robert Hedgpeth 2021
R. Hedgpeth, *R2DBC Revealed*, https://doi.org/10.1007/978-1-4842-6989-3_3

There are other commonalities, of course, like the ability to execute queries, manage transactions, and so on, but there are also many differences between database solutions. For instance, consider support for specific data types, like Binary Large and Character Large Objects (BLOB, CLOB) which don't exist in every database. In order to work with the underlying database, using those types, the driver would need to implement specific support.

Why am I mentioning this? Why is this important? Well, the takeaway is that there are pieces of functionality that some databases either cannot or choose not to support. The R2DBC specification has been created to establish a baseline, or standard, among all relational databases and not to be so overreaching in that it becomes overly opinionated or too focused, thereby adding more complexity for some drivers (Figure 3-1).

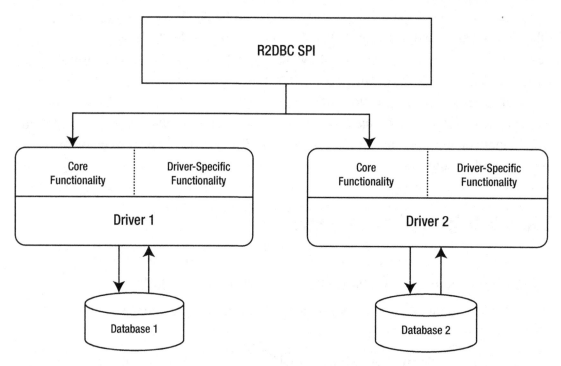

***Figure 3-1.*** *R2DBC provides the ability for implementations to use shared and driver-specific functionality*

---

**Note**    Drivers have a large amount of flexibility when implementing the R2DBC specification, including using different Reactive Streams API implementations like Project Reactor, RxJava, and others.

---

# Power in Simplicity

R2DBC drivers must fully implement the database wire protocol on top of a non-blocking I/O layer, but, beyond that, the technological landscape is wide open. Having the hindsight of previous connectivity standards, like JDBC, R2DBC seeks to remain agnostic to the specific technologies. As you know, this is possible because R2DBC is merely a collection of interfaces, lacking any actual implementation content.

Ultimately, drivers must supply all implemented content, using R2DBC as a sort of blueprint. Within that blueprint is the usage of the Reactive Streams API as another blueprint that also needs an implementation.

For instance, remember that Reactive Streams specifies an interface for `Publisher`:

```
public interface Publisher<T> {
    public void subscribe(Subscriber<? super T> s);
}
```

This is important; because, as you'll learn in future chapters, of R2DBC's focus on non-blocking behavior, some methods don't return values directly.

Take, for example, R2DBC's `ConnectionFactory` interface:

```
package io.r2dbc.spi;
import org.reactivestreams.Publisher;
public interface ConnectionFactory {
    Publisher<? extends Connection> create();
    ConnectionFactoryMetadata getMetadata();
}
```

Notice that the process of creating a new `Connection` doesn't return a new Connection object directly. Instead, the create method returns a *promise* of a `Connection` object that can be used when it's received, at some unknown time in the future. This is how the driver is able to utilize the concept of back pressure, bringing it all full circle!

---

**Note**   I'll dive into more details regarding the connection specifications, guidelines, and interfaces in Chapter 4.

---

As you can imagine, these types of *declarative* workflows create ample opportunities for underlying implementations. In fact, there are a variety of options to choose from. The Reactive Streams specification can be implemented from scratch, or there are a variety of existing implementations (e.g., Project Reactor, Reactor Netty, RxJava) available. Every driver has the freedom to implement as it sees fit (Figure 3-2).

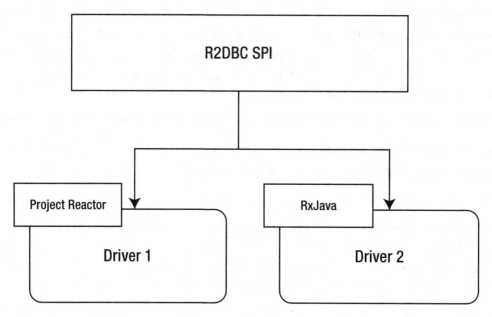

***Figure 3-2.***  *Possible driver technology variations*

# R2DBC Compliance

Up until this point, the process by which drivers can implement the R2DBC specification has been described generally, but in order to be considered truly compliant, drivers must satisfy specific criteria.

# Guiding Principles

According to the R2DBC documentation, there are a collection of guidelines and requirements that must be satisfied by all drivers, which are listed as follows:

– The R2DBC SPI should implement SQL support as its primary interface. R2DBC does not rely upon, nor presume, a specific SQL version. SQL and aspects of statements can be entirely handled in the data source or as part of the driver.

- The specification consists of the official R2DBC specification documentation and the specifications documented in each interface's Javadoc. The Javadocs are available at `http://r2dbc.io/spec/`.

- Drivers that support parameterized statements must also support bind parameter markers.

- Drivers that support parameterized statements must also support at least one parameter binding method, by index or name.

- Drivers must support database transactions.

- Index references to columns and parameters are zero-based. That is, the first index begins with 0.

Ultimately, these requirements serve as a road map to achieving *official* compliance with the R2DBC specification and broadly describe what is expected of any driver implementation.

# Specification Implementation Requirements

As you'll come to learn in subsequent chapters, there are many interfaces within the R2DBC specification that can be implemented within drivers, but not all of them are required to be. At least, not in full. This harkens back to the differences between database solutions and allows for a broad range of flexibility for each driver to be able to tap into the unique functionality and capabilities that it provides.

For starters, all drivers are required to

- Implement a non-blocking I/O layer. In other words, all communication within the driver to the target database must be completely non-blocking and adhering to the values of reactive programming (e.g., providing a functioning and compliant Reactive Streams implementation).

- Support `ConnectionFactory` discovery through the *Java Service Loader* of `ConnectionFactoryProvider`.

---

**Note**   The Java Service Loader, or, more specifically, the `ServiceLoader` class, functions to discover and load service implementations lazily. It uses the context classpath to locate service provider implementations and put them in an internal cache.

---

Beyond those two general requirements and as indicated by the R2DBC specification documentation, there exist requirements for implementation of individual interfaces. All of the interfaces need to be fully or partially implemented.

All drivers must fully implement the following interfaces:

- `io.r2dbc.spi.ConnectionFactory`

- `io.r2dbc.spi.ConnectionFactoryMetadata`

- `io.r2dbc.spi.ConnectionFactoryProvider`

- `io.r2dbc.spi.Result`

- `io.r2dbc.spi.Row`

- `io.r2dbc.spi.RowMetadata`

- `io.r2dbc.spi.Batch`

All drivers must partially implement the following interfaces:

- Implement the `io.r2dbc.spi.Connection` interface, except for the following optional methods:

  - `createSavepoint`: Calling this method should throw an `UnsupportedOperations` exception for drivers that do not support savepoints.

  - `releaseSavepoint`: Calling this method should be a no-op for drivers that do not support savepoint release.

---

**Note**   A no operation, or no-op, is a computer instruction that takes up a small amount of space but specifies no operation. Practically speaking, this is a method that functions as a placeholder and does nothing.

---

- `rollbackTransactionToSavepoint`: Calling this method should throw an `UnsupportedOperations` exception for drivers that do not support savepoints.

---

**Note**    Savepoints provide a fine-grained control mechanism by marking intermediate points within a transaction. Once a savepoint has been created, a transaction can be rolled back to that savepoint without affecting preceding work.

---

- Implement the `io.r2dbc.spi.Statement` interface, except for the following optional methods:

- `returnGeneratedValues`: Calling this method should be a no operation (no-op) for drivers that do not support key generation.

- `fetchSize`: Calling this method should be a no-op for drivers that do not support fetch size hints.

- Implement the `io.r2dbc.spi.ColumnMetadata` interface, except for the following optional methods:

- `getPrecision`

- `getScale`

- `getNullability`

- `getJavaType`

- `getNativeTypeMetadata`

# Specification Extensions

Drivers also have the option of using extensions to the core R2DBC interfaces. Extensions can be used to supplement specification interfaces to provide features that are not required for R2DBC implementation.

# Wrapped Interfaces

The R2DBC specification contains an interface called Wrapped, as shown in Listing 3-1, that provides instances a way of accessing resources that have been wrapped. It also allows R2DBC implementations the ability to expose wrapped resources.

***Listing 3-1.*** The Wrapped interface

```
public interface Wrapped<T> {
    T unwrap();
}
```

---

**Note**    The unwrap method can be used to return an object that implements the specified interface, allowing access to vendor-specific methods.

---

R2DBC SPI wrappers can be created by implementing the Wrapped interface, making it possible for callers to extract the original instance. Any R2DBC SPI interface can be wrapped. Consider the following example of wrapping a Connection, as shown in Listing 3-2.

***Listing 3-2.*** A Wrapped interface implementation example.

```
class ConnectionWrapper implements Connection, Wrapped<Connection> {
    private final Connection wrapped;
    @Override
    public Connection unwrap() {
        return this.wrapped;
    }
    // Construction and implementation details omitted for brevity.
}
```

# Closeable Interfaces

The R2DBC specification contains an interface called Closeable, as shown in Listing 3-3, that provides a way for objects to release associated resources that are no longer being used in a non-blocking fashion.

***Listing 3-3.*** The Closable interface

```
import org.reactivestreams.Publisher;
import org.reactivestreams.Subscriber;

@FunctionalInterface
public interface Closeable {
    Publisher<Void> close();
}
```

---

**Note**    The close method is used to return a Publisher to start the close operation and get notified upon completion. If the object is already closed, then subscriptions complete successfully, and the close operation has no effect.

---

Closable objects are required to implement the Closeable interface. Once instantiated, a caller can use the close option, from Closeable, on any obtained Publisher objects and will be notified upon completion.

Take, for example, the Connection interface that extends the Closeable interface, as shown Listing 3-4.

***Listing 3-4.*** A Closable interface usage example

```
import org.reactivestreams.Publisher;
public interface Connection extends Closeable {

...

}
```

Here, Connection is an instantiated object implementing the Connection interface. Then, as indicated in Listing 3-5, because the Connection interface extends the Closeable interface, the close function is able to be used.

***Listing 3-5.*** Using a close method implementation

```
Publisher<Void> close = connection.close();
```

# Testing and Validation

The process for claiming a driver as R2DBC compliant is informal. In fact, so informal that anyone can claim that they've created an R2DBC driver. Aside from the documentation guidelines I've previously indicated, there is only a small Test Compatibility Kit (TCK) that lives within the R2DBC repository on GitHub. And at the time I'm writing this, the TCK is fairly lightweight and contains basic tests. All testing and compliance efforts rest solely on the driver's developers.

# Summary

In this chapter, I reviewed the high-level process of creating an R2DBC driver. You learned that the R2DBC specification was created in a way to strike a balance between standardization of core relational database interactions in a reactive manner and providing a high degree of flexibility and extensibility that enable creation of robust drivers.

This chapter has helped set the stage for upcoming chapters where we'll be diving deeper into the capabilities of the R2DBC specification, which will help you gain more insight into how R2DBC driver implementations come together.

# CHAPTER 4

# Connections

Supporting connections to data sources is an important piece of functionality within any application. In fact, depending on the application, it may very well be the *most important* piece of functionality. Understanding the significance of the connection functionality, the R2DBC specification provides a variety of interfaces and classes that allow driver implementations to not only establish connections but efficiently manage them in a purely reactive manner.

   In this chapter, I'll examine the *most crucial* aspect of the R2DBC SPI, creating and managing connections. I'll dive into the hierarchy of entities available within the API to expand on how they're designed and come together to provide an extremely robust and flexible solution for implementing drivers.

## Establishing Connections

Ultimately, everything culminates to the Connection interface, which R2DBC uses to define a connection API to underlying data sources. For the most part, the target data source is likely to be a relational database that uses SQL as its data access method, but, as I've previously pointed out, it isn't a hard requirement. However, for our purposes and in this chapter, I'll be focusing on connections specifically targeting relational database management systems (RDMSs).

---

**Note** R2DBC driver implementations aren't required to use relational databases as their underlying data source and can, in fact, use any data source, including stream-oriented and object-oriented systems.

---

© Robert Hedgpeth 2021
R. Hedgpeth, *R2DBC Revealed*, https://doi.org/10.1007/978-1-4842-6989-3_4

# The Anatomy

Over the course of time, applications that use database connections often need to manage more than one, possibly even many connections. The R2DBC SPI makes it possible for applications to manage connections to one or more data sources. While the intention of a `Connection` object is to enable drivers to establish and maintain a single client connection, applications often require more complexity than that.

But because a `Connection` object represents a single client session and has associated state information, such as user identification and what transaction semantics are in effect, `Connection` objects are not safe for concurrent state-changing interactions by multiple subscribers.

In fact, it's even possible for `Connection` objects to be shared across multiple threads that serially run operations by using appropriate synchronization mechanisms.

Luckily, rather than requiring applications to create and manage `Connection` objects directly, R2DBC drivers make it possible for connections to be safely and securely obtained by

1. Using a `ConnectionFactory` implementation to create a `Connection` object

2. Using the `ConnectionFactories` class, provided by R2DBC, by utilizing one or more `ConnectionFactoryProvider` implementations which can then be used to obtain a `ConnectionFactory` implementation

Later in this chapter, we'll dive deeper into connection factories and the role they play in the relationships between the various other connection classes and interfaces. But for now, let's keep our focus on the path to creating a connection through the use of connection factories (Figure 4-1).

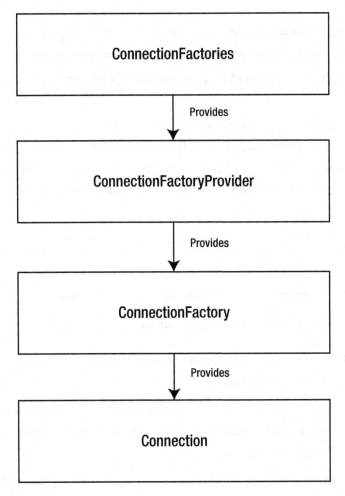

**Figure 4-1.** *The R2DBC connection hierarchy*

# R2DBC Hindsight

If you've ever worked with the JDBC API, you know that it can be an involved and, often, frustrating process. Over the years, JDBC has become very opinionated, requiring developers to adhere to its underlying technology and functional constraints.

You've learned that R2DBC was created to provide a high level of flexibility for driver implementations to allow them to tap into unique features and functionality of their targeted data sources. And, at the same time, R2DBC aims to standardize capabilities required by all drivers. A practical example of this is the use of a standard Uniform Resource Locator (URL) format.

**Note**   A database connection URL is a string that JDBC drivers use to connect to a database. It can contain information such as where to search for the database, the name of the database to connect to, and many other configuration options.

In contrast to JDBC, which requires each driver implementation to create requirements, including URL parsing workflows, R2DBC defines a standard URL format. The format is an enhanced form of Request for Comments (RFC) 3986 Uniform Resource Identifier (URI): Generic Syntax, and its amendments are supported by Java's `java.net.URI` type.

*Figure 4-2.*  *The R2DBC connection URL format*

Creating a URL standard allows all driver implementations to uniformly take advantage of the following configuration options:

- `scheme`: Identifies that the URL is a valid R2DBC URL. There are two valid schemes, *r2dbc* and *r2dbcs*, which are used to configure Secure Sockets Layer (SSL) usage.

- `driver`: Identifies a specific driver implementation (e.g., MySQL, MariaDB, etc.).

- `protocol`: An optional parameter used to configure a driver-specific protocol. Protocols can be organized hierarchically and are separated by a colon (:).

- `authority`: Contains an endpoint and authorization. The authority may contain a single host or a collection of hostnames and port tuples by separating these with a comma (,).

- `path`: (optional) Used as an initial schema or database name.

- `query`: (optional) Used to pass additional configuration options in the form of string key-value pairs by using the key name as the option name.

# Connection Factory

In computer science, a factory is as an object that creates other objects. This is useful, because in class-based programming, a factory functions as an abstraction for the constructor of the target object, which helps localize the instantiation of a complex object (Figure 4-3).

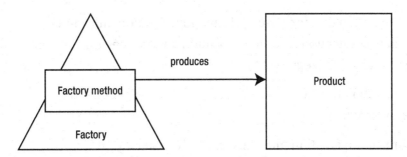

***Figure 4-3.***  *A Factory object workflow*

Tapping into this approach, the R2DBC `ConnectionFactory` interface provides the blueprint for drivers to create objects that are responsible for the creation of `Connection` objects (Listing 4-1).

***Listing 4-1.***  The R2DBC ConnectionFactory interface

```
import org.reactivestreams.Publisher;
public interface ConnectionFactory {
    Publisher<? extends Connection> create();
    ConnectionFactoryMetadata getMetadata();
}
```

# Driver Implementations

Using a factory-based approach to facilitate connection creation and management allows drivers to abstract away the vendor-specific, or database-specific, aspects in an effort to create a simpler, more streamlined application development experience.

Drilling deeper, the R2DBC documentation indicates a number of requirements that define exactly *what* `ConnectionFactory` implementations must accomplish to be considered viable:

1. A ConnectionFactory represents a resource factory for deferred connection creation. It may create connections by itself, wrap a ConnectionFactory, or apply connection pooling on top of a ConnectionFactory.

2. A ConnectionFactory provides metadata about the driver itself through ConnectionFactoryMetadata.

3. A ConnectionFactory uses deferred initialization and should initiate connection resource allocation after requesting the item (Subscription.request(1)).

4. Connection creation must emit exactly one Connection or an error signal.

5. Connection creation must be cancellable (Subscription. cancel()). Canceling connection creation must release ("close") the connection and all associated resources.

6. A ConnectionFactory should expect that it can be wrapped. Wrappers must implement the Wrapped<ConnectionFactory> interface and return the underlying ConnectionFactory when Wrapped.unwrap() gets called.

## Exposing Metadata

The ConnectionFactory interface includes a function called getMetadata that requires class implementations to provide metadata to identify the name of the target product (Listing 4-2).

*Listing 4-2.* The ConnectionFactoryMetadata interface

```
public interface ConnectionFactoryMetadata {
String getName();
}
```

# ConnectionFactories

Providing additional abstraction, the SPI also contains a fully implemented class called ConnectionFactories, which exists to eliminate the need for application developers to implement Connection discovery functionality. The ConnectionFactories discovery mechanism makes it possible to automatically find and load any R2DBC driver found on the *classpath* through the use of Java's ServiceLoader mechanism and the ConnectionFactoryProvider interface.

## Discovery

ConnectionFactoryProvider is a Java service interface that, when implemented, provides the ability to examine the ConnectionFactoryOptions class (Listing 4-3).

*Listing 4-3.* The ConnectionFactoryProvider interface

```
import java.util.ServiceLoader;
public interface ConnectionFactoryProvider {
ConnectionFactory create(ConnectionFactoryOptions
connectionFactoryOptions);
boolean supports(ConnectionFactoryOptions connectionFactoryOptions);
String getDriver();
}
```

The ConnectionFactoryOptions class represents a configuration for a request of a ConnectionFactory object from a ConnectionFactoryProvider object (Figure 4-4).

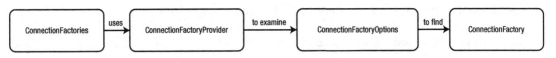

*Figure 4-4.* *The high-level ConnectionFactory discovery workflow*

# Bringing It All Together

Using ConnectionFactoryProvider objects, the ConnectionFactories class provides two methods for bootstrapping a ConnectionFactory object:

1. Using an R2DBC connection URL. The URL string will then be parsed in order to create a ConnectionFactoryOptions object.

***Listing 4-4.*** Obtaining a ConnectionFactory using an R2DBC URL

```
ConnectionFactory factory = ConnectionFactories.get("r2dbc:a-
driver:pipes://localhost:3306/my_database?locale=en_US");
```

2. Programmatically by building a ConnectionFactoryOptions object directly.

***Listing 4-5.*** Obtaining a ConnectionFactory using ConnectionFactoryOptions programmatically

```
ConnectionFactoryOptions options = ConnectionFactoryOptions.builder()
    .option(ConnectionFactoryOptions.DRIVER, "a-driver")
    .option(ConnectionFactoryOptions.PROTOCOL, "pipes")
    .option(ConnectionFactoryOptions.HOST, "localhost")
    .option(ConnectionFactoryOptions.PORT, 3306)
    .option(ConnectionFactoryOptions.DATABASE, "my_database")
    .option(Option.valueOf("locale"), "en_US")
    .build();

ConnectionFactory factory = ConnectionFactories.get(options);
```

Once you've obtained a ConnectionFactory object, you'll have the ability to obtain a Connection object.

# Connections

Each connection implementation instantiation of the Connection interface (Listing 4-6) provides a single connection to a database.

*Listing 4-6.* The R2DBC Connection interface

```
import org.reactivestreams.Publisher;
public interface Connection extends Closeable {
    Publisher<Void> beginTransaction();
    @Override Publisher<Void> close();
    Publisher<Void> commitTransaction();
    Batch createBatch();
    Publisher<Void> createSavepoint(String name);
    Statement createStatement(String sql);
    boolean isAutoCommit();
    ConnectionMetadata getMetadata();
    IsolationLevel getTransactionIsolationLevel();
    Publisher<Void> releaseSavepoint(String name);
    Publisher<Void> rollbackTransaction();
    Publisher<Void> rollbackTransactionToSavepoint(String name);
    Publisher<Void> setAutoCommit(boolean autoCommit);
    Publisher<Void> setTransactionIsolationLevel(IsolationLevel
    isolationLevel);
    Publisher<Boolean> validate(ValidationDepth depth);
}
```

---

**Tip**   Notice that the `Connection` interface utilizes the Reactive Streams API for many of the functions' return types to be provided as type `Publisher`. Harkening back to Chapter 2, remember that a *publisher* functions as a promise of a response, or result, at an unknown time in the future.

---

When a connection is established, using the `Connection` object, SQL statements can then be executed and results subsequently returned. And according to the R2DBC documentation, a `Connection` object can consist of any number of transport connections to the underlying database or represent a session over a multiplexed transport connection. For maximum portability, connections should be used synchronously.

Ultimately, `Connection` objects exist to initiate database conversations, transaction management, and statement execution.

***Table 4-1.***  *The Connection interface functions*

| Name | Description |
|---|---|
| beginTransaction | Begins a new transaction. Calling this method will disable auto-commit mode. |
| close | Releases any resources held by the Connection object. |
| commitTransaction | Commits the current transaction. |
| createBatch | Creates a new batch (see Chapter 8). |
| createSavePoint | Creates a new savepoint in the current transaction. |
| createStatement | Creates a new statement for building a statement-based (SQL) request. |
| isAutoCommit | Returns the auto-commit mode for the connection. |
| getMetadata | Returns the ConnectionMetaData about the product (e.g., MariaDB database) that the connection is connected to. |
| getTransactionIsolationLevel | Returns the IsolationLevel for the connection. |
| releaseSavePoint | Releases a savepoint in the current transaction. |
| rollbackTransaction | Rolls back the current transaction. |
| rollbackTransactionToSavepoint | Rolls back the current transaction to a savepoint. |
| setAutoCommit | Configures the auto-commit mode for the current transaction. |
| setTransactionIsolationLevel | Configures the isolation level for the current transaction. |
| validate | Validates the connection according to the given ValidationDepth. |

# Obtaining Connections

Connection objects can only be created and acquired through a ConnectionFactory object, which I previously elaborated on. Once you've obtained a ConnectionFactory object, you can use the create method to access a connection.

***Listing 4-7.*** Creating a connection from a ConnectionFactory object

```
Publisher<? extends Connection> publisher = factory.create();
```

# Acquiring Metadata

The R2DBC specification requires that connections expose metadata about the databases they are connected to by implementing the ConnectionMetadata interface (Listing 4-8).

***Listing 4-8.*** ConnectionMetadata interface

```
public interface ConnectionMetadata {
    String getDatabaseProductName();
    String getDatabaseVersion();
}
```

---

**Note**    The information found within a ConnectionMetadata object is typically discovered dynamically based on the information acquired at the initialization of a connection.

---

# Validating Connections

Once a Connection object has been instantiated, the validate method can be used to obtain a status of the connection. The validate method accepts a ValidationDepth argument, which indicates the depth to which the connection should be validated.

ValidationDepth is an enumeration that contains two constants:

- ValidationDepth.LOCAL: Indicated to perform a client-side-only validation.

- ValidationDepth.REMOTE: Indicated to perform remote connection validation.

## Closing Connections

Looking back at the Connection interface, you'll notice that it implements the Closable interface (Listing 4-9).

*Listing 4-9.* The Closeable interface

```
import org.reactivestreams.Publisher;
import org.reactivestreams.Subscriber;

@FunctionalInterface
public interface Closeable {
    Publisher<Void> close();
}
```

The Closable interface exposes a method called close that, when invoked, will release any resources that the implementing object, Connection in this case, is holding.

*Listing 4-10.* Closing a connection

```
Publisher<Void> close = connection.close();
```

## Summary

Providing the ability to connect to an underlying data source is one of the most important capabilities of the R2DBC specification. While sharing many similarities, relational databases can also contain distinct connection requirements. Using only a small collection of interfaces and classes, R2DBC is able to provide common functionality shared among all data sources as well as provide the flexibility for drivers to incorporate the unique features of their target product.

All of the information you've learned in this chapter will help you in the chapters to come. After all, without the ability to connect, it'd end up being a pretty short book.

# CHAPTER 5

# Transactions

The ability to support transactions is a crucial aspect of all relational databases. In fact, it's one of their *most* important features as their usage is often a crucial part of maintaining databases of any size and complexity.

Given that understanding, it makes sense that the R2DBC specification provides support and guidance for driver implementations to expose core transactional management capabilities. Along the way, we'll explore what transactional features the specification requires to be implemented while also examining how and when they can be utilized. All this in an effort to learn how R2DBC helps utilize transactions in order to provide data integrity, isolation, correct application semantics, and a consistent view of data during reactive, concurrent database access.

## Transaction Fundamentals

Before diving into the details of how the R2DBC specification handles transactions, it's important to understand the fundamentals concepts, requirements, and usages of transactional management within relational databases, if only to refresh your existing knowledge.

*Transactions* are defined as logical units of work that contain one or more SQL statements (Figure 5-1).

© Robert Hedgpeth 2021
R. Hedgpeth, *R2DBC Revealed*, https://doi.org/10.1007/978-1-4842-6989-3_5

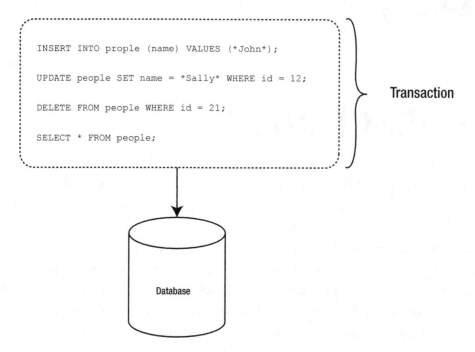

```
INSERT INTO prople (name) VALUES (*John*);

UPDATE people SET name = *Sally* WHERE id = 12;

DELETE FROM people WHERE id = 21;

SELECT * FROM people;
```

Transaction

Database

**Figure 5-1.**  *A transaction contains one or more SQL statements, initiated as a single unit of work*

Put more simply, you can think of transactions as the propagation of one or more changes to a database.

## The Need for Transactions

But to understand *why* grouping SQL statements as transactions is necessary, let's first consider a simple, relatable scenario. Take, for example, the process of transferring money from one bank account to another, and, for the sake of simplicity, let's imagine that this process involves simply updating the balances (Listing 5-1).

**Listing 5-1.**  A sample update to account tables using SQL

```
UPDATE savings_account SET balance = 0 WHERE account_id = 1;
UPDATE checking_account SET balance = 100 WHERE account_id = 1;
```

Of course, as you can imagine, it's important that the money is where you expect it to be, when you expect it to be there. That means that the changes to each account must either both succeed or both fail. Otherwise, you'd be left with money being removed from, or added to, one account and not the other, creating a mismatch of information. In database management systems, supporting these types of expectations is known as *ACID compliance*.

## ACID Compliance

As I previously defined, transactions are units of work, but, expanding on that, transactions are more specifically known as *atomic* units of work. This means that when a transaction makes one or many changes to the database, either all of the changes succeed when the transaction is committed, or all the changes are undone when the transaction is rolled back. This "all or nothing" property is known as **atomicity**.

A transaction is intended to be a single, isolated unit, and, as such, operations executed within it cannot be merged with other database operations that aren't involved in the process. However, because transactions can consist of multiple SQL commands, possibly even accessing multiple databases, it's important that database management systems ensure that the operations happen without interference from other database commands that might be running at the same time, or concurrently. This is a characteristic property known as **isolation**.

To ensure that the database system does not miss a successfully completed transaction from a later failure, the actions of a transaction must persist between failures. In addition, the results of one transaction can only be undone by another transaction. This property is known as **durability**.

Because of these three properties, the role of a transaction is to preserve database consistency, through a property aptly known as **consistency**.

These properties come together to form the acronym ACID, as summarized in Figure 5-2.

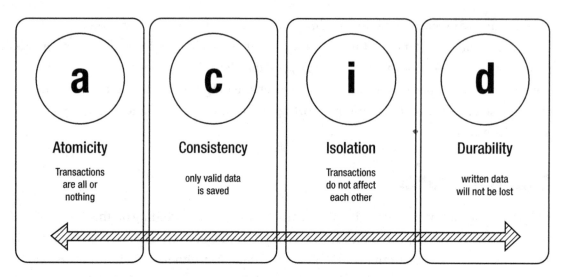

***Figure 5-2.*** *A high-level summary of ACID properties*

## Methods of Control

In practice, transactions start with the first executable SQL statement and end when they're either committed or rolled back (Figure 5-3).

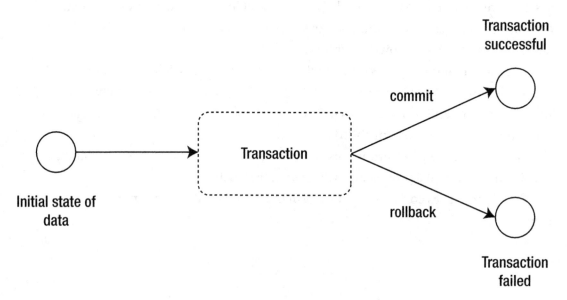

***Figure 5-3.*** *A simple transactional workflow*

---

**Caution**    Not all SQL statements are able to be rolled back for all database management systems. MySQL and MariaDB, for example, do not support rolling back modifications such as data description language (DDL), the syntax for creating and modifying database objects such as tables, indexes, and users. Please check the documentation of your target database for more information.

---

## Committing Transactions

*Committing* a transaction is the process of permanently saving the changes to the database (Listing 5-2).

*Listing 5-2.*  Committing a MariaDB transaction using SQL

```
START TRANSACTION;
UPDATE savings_account SET balance = 0 WHERE account_id = 1;
UPDATE checking_account SET balance = 100 WHERE account_id = 1;
COMMIT;
```

## Rolling Back Transactions

*Rolling back* a transaction means undoing any changes to the data within an uncommitted transaction. Transactions are rolled back automatically if an error occurs when executing SQL within the transaction scope, but they can also be rolled back manually as seen in Listing 5-3.

*Listing 5-3.*  Rolling back a MariaDB transaction using SQL

```
START TRANSACTION;
UPDATE savings_account SET balance = 0 WHERE account_id = 1;
UPDATE checking_account SET balance = 100 WHERE account_id = 1;
ROLLBACK;
```

### Savepoints

Many relational databases also support *savepoints,* a named sub-transaction. Savepoints provide the ability to mark intermediate points within a transaction that can be rolled back to without affecting preceding work (Listing 5-4).

***Listing 5-4.*** Rolling back to a MariaDB savepoint using SQL

```
START TRANSACTION;
UPDATE savings_account SET balance = 0 WHERE account_id = 1;
SAVEPOINT savings_account_updated;
UPDATE checking_account SET balance = 100 WHERE account_id = 1;
ROLLBACK TO SAVEPOINT savings_account_updated;
```

# R2DBC Transaction Management

The R2DBC specification provides support for controlling transactional operations via code, as opposed to using SQL directly, through the Connection interface, which all drivers are required to implement.

## Auto-commit Mode

Transactions can be started implicitly or explicitly. When a Connection object is in auto-commit mode, which is examined in more detail later on in this chapter, transactions are started implicitly when a SQL statement is executed through a Connection object.

---

**Stay Tuned**    In Chapter 6, we will discover how SQL statements can be prepared and executed using the Connection object.

---

The Connection object provides two methods of interacting with the auto-commit mode as indicated in Table 5-1.

***Table 5-1.*** *Connection object methods used to view and edit transaction auto-commit functionality*

| Method | Return Type | Description |
|---|---|---|
| setAutoCommit | Publisher<Void> | Configures the auto-commit mode for the current transaction. |
| isAutoCommit | boolean | Returns the auto-commit mode for the transaction. The default value for isAutoCommit is determined by the driver implementation. |

As indicated within the R2DBC specification documentation, applications should change the auto-commit mode by invoking the setAutoCommit method instead of executing SQL commands to change the underlying connection configuration. If, for whatever reason, the value of auto-commit is changed during an active transaction, the current transaction is committed.

---

**Caution**   If the setAutoCommit method is called and the value for auto-commit has not changed from its current value, it will be treated as a no-op.

---

Know that modifying a Connection object's auto-commit mode will most likely, depending on the implementation, initiate some kind of action on the underlying database, which is why setAutoCommit returns a Publisher object. In contrast, using isAutoCommit will typically involve using the driver's state instead of having to communicate with the database.

# Explicit Transactions

However, when auto-commit mode is disabled, transactions must be explicitly started. This can be accomplished by invoking the beginTransaction method on a Connection object.

*Listing 5-5.* Creating a publisher to begin a transaction

```
Publisher<Void> begin = connection.beginTransaction();
```

## Committing Transactions

Once a transaction has been started explicitly, it must also be explicitly committed.

*Listing 5-6.* Creating a publisher to commit a transaction

```
Publisher<Void> commit = connection.commitTransaction();
```

## Rolling Back Transactions

If, for some reason, one of the queries being executed by a transaction fails, they can all be rolled back using the rollbackTransaction method.

***Listing 5-7.*** Handling an error with a committed transaction and rolling back

```
try {
    Publisher<Void> begin = connection.beginTransaction();
    Publisher<Void> updateSavings = connection.createStatement("UPDATE
savings_account SET balance = 0 WHERE account_id = 1").execute();
    Publisher<Void> updateChecking = connection.createStatement("UPDATE
checking_account SET balance = 100 WHERE account_id = 1").execute();
    Publisher<Void> transaction = connection.commitTransaction();
}
catch (SQLException ex) {
    Publisher<Void> transaction = connection.rollbackTransaction();
}
```

---

**Tip**   Notice that I've provided examples for creating `Publisher` objects. However, in order for a `Publisher`'s functionality to be executed, it must be subscribed to. In order for a `Publisher` object to be subscribed to, it must have an official R2DBC implementation. To see this in action, take a look at the pragmatic R2DBC driver examples provided in Chapter 14.

---

# Managing Savepoints

The `Connection` interface provides three methods, indicated in Table 5-2, that can be used to manage savepoints.

***Table 5-2.*** *Connection object methods used to manage savepoints*

| Method | Return Type | Description |
| --- | --- | --- |
| createSavepoint() | Publisher<Void> | Creates a savepoint in the current transaction. |
| releaseSavepoint() | Publisher<Void> | Releases a savepoint in the current transaction. |
| rollbackTransactionToSavepoint (String name) | Publisher<Void> | Rolls back to a savepoint in the current transaction. |

**The `createSavepoint` method can be used to set a savepoint within the scope of a transaction. If there is no active transaction, a transaction will be started if `createSavepoint` is invoked.**

---

**Note**   Creating savepoints within a transaction will disable auto-commit for the containing connection.

---

After a savepoint has been created, the `rollbackTransactionToSavepoint` method can be used to roll back work, without rolling back the entire transaction.

***Listing 5-8.*** Rolling back a transaction to a savepoint.

```
Publisher<Void> begin = connection.beginTransaction();
Publisher<Void> updateSavings = connection.createStatement("UPDATE savings_
account SET balance = 0 WHERE account_id = 1").execute();
Publisher<Void> savepoint = connection.createSavepoint("savepoint");
Publisher<Void> updateChecking = connection.createStatement("UPDATE
checking_account SET balance = 100 WHERE account_id = 1").execute();
Publisher<Void> partialRollback = connection.rollbackTransactionToSavepoint
("savepoint");
Publisher<Void> commit = connection.commitTransaction();
```

---

**Note**   According to the R2DBC specification documentation, drivers that do not support savepoint creation and rolling back to a savepoint will throw an `UnsupportedOperationException` to indicate that those features are not supported.

---

# Releasing Savepoints

It's important to note that savepoints allocate resources directly on the databases. Because of this, some database vendors may require that savepoints be released to dispose of resources.

Using the `releaseSavepoint` method will release savepoints that are no longer needed. Savepoints will also be released if

- A transaction is committed.

- A transaction is completely rolled back.

- A transaction is rolled back to that savepoint.

- A transaction is rolled back to a preceding savepoint.

Calling the `releaseSavepoint` method within driver implementations that do not support savepoint release functionality will result in a no-op, according the R2DBC specification documentation.

# Isolation Levels

Databases expose the ability to specify the level of isolation within transactions. The concept of transactional isolation defines the degree to which one transaction can be isolated from data or resource modification performed by other transactions, thereby impacting concurrent access while multiple transactions are active.

## Managing Isolation

The R2DBC specification contains a class called `IsolationLevel` that is used to represent the isolation level constant for a given `Connection`. Using a `Connection` object, you can utilize an `IsolationLevel` object to get and set the transaction isolation level with `getTransactionIsolationLevel` and `setTransactionIsolationLevel`, respectively.

The IsolationLevel class contains four isolation level constants, which are defined by the ANSI/ISO SQL standard and are listed as follows:

- **READ_COMMITTED:** A lock-based concurrency control DBMS implementation keeps write locks until the end of a transaction. Read locks, however, are released as soon as a SELECT operation is performed.

- **READ_UNCOMMITTED:** Dirty reads are allowed, so no one transaction may see changes that have yet to be committed by other transactions. This is the *lowest* level of isolation.

- **REPEATABLE_READ:** A locked-based concurrency control DBMS implementation keeps read and write locks until the end of the transaction. In this level, phantom reads, which are when new rows are added or removed by another transaction to or from the records currently being read, are allowed to occur.

- **SERIALIZABLE**: A lock-based concurrency control DBMS implementation requires read and write locks to be released at the end of a transaction. In this level, phantom reads are avoided. This is the *highest* level of isolation.

## Performance Considerations

Note that changing the transaction isolation level can negatively impact performance. As indicated in the preceding text, within the IsolationLevel options, databases will typically modify the amount of locking and resource overhead used to ensure isolation level semantics.

Depending on the availability of concurrent access that is supported at any given time may impact application performance. With that in mind, the R2DBC specification documentation recommends that transaction management functionality be responsible for weighing the need for data consistency against the requirements for performance when determining which transaction isolation level is appropriate.

# Summary

In this chapter, we examined the fundamentals of transactions. We learned or refreshed our memories on the basic anatomy of transactions, control mechanisms, and why they are necessary. We also learned that the R2DBC specification supports starting and managing transactions, targeting core transactional features and capabilities shared across ACID-compliant databases. Along the way we gained an understanding of how to leverage R2DBC transactional capabilities within our own code. In addition, we were introduced to the complexities of transactional isolation levels and their support within the specification.

# CHAPTER 6

# Statements

You learned in the previous chapter that establishing a connection to the database is one of the most crucial requirements of a database driver. And while that's certainly true, merely connecting to a database isn't all that useful to your application if you can't send and receive information to and from the underlying data store.

In this chapter, we're going to take a look at how we can create and execute SQL statements using R2DBC. We'll start by examining the basic hierarchy of objects and the workflow involved in facilitating back-and-forth interaction with a database using R2DBC. Then, having gained a better understanding of the core pieces of functionality, we'll take a look at the more complex features.

## SQL Statements

As you know, database engines are essentially just data repositories, containing the data necessary for external needs, like applications. The repositories themselves may contain a variety of structures and mechanisms used to organize the data. Every relational database vendor has different organizational mechanisms ranging from subtle to very distinct. At the end of the day, they all rely on one standard to wrangle it all: SQL.

But diving into the gritty details of how relational databases optimize, parse, and execute SQL is, ultimately, out of scope for what we're looking to examine in this book. Instead, we should focus on the general gist, that SQL statements are sent to the database and a result, of some sort, is expected.

© Robert Hedgpeth 2021
R. Hedgpeth, *R2DBC Revealed*, https://doi.org/10.1007/978-1-4842-6989-3_6

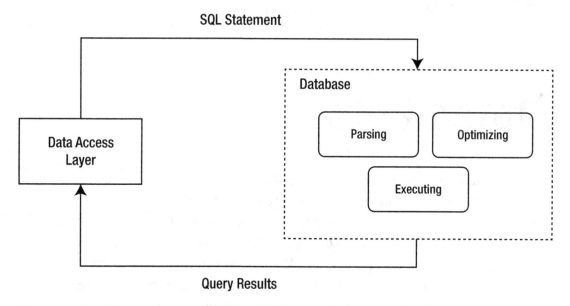

***Figure 6-1.*** *A basic database/SQL workflow*

# R2DBC Statements

Aside from connecting to an underlying data source, executing SQL statements is likely to be one of the most prevalent uses of an R2DBC driver.

The Connection object is responsible for creating and managing the Statement objects that will be used to acquire query results from the database (Figure 6-2).

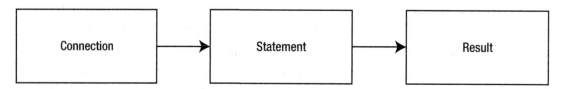

***Figure 6-2.*** *The class flow for executing SQL statements with R2DBC*

The R2DBC Statement interface defines methods for inputting, organizing, and executing SQL statements. The Statement interface facilitates two methods of statement creation and execution: non-parameterized and parameterized.

Unlike the JDBC specification, which provides Statement and PreparedStatement objects, R2DBC only relies on a single object implementation to accommodate the creation and execution of both general and parameter-determined SQL statements. Ultimately, the driver implementation must contain the functionality to determine what kind of statement to execute.

# The Basics

As previously noted, SQL statement interactions on underlying databases are facilitated through the use of Statement objects. In the simplest case, fully self-contained, static SQL statements can be used to create Statement objects.

## Creating Statements

The Connection object exposes a method called createStatement that returns a new Statement object. The createStatement method accepts a single string value that must contain valid SQL (Listing 6-1).

***Listing 6-1.*** Creating a statement using the Connection object

```
Statement statement = connection.createStatement("SELECT title FROM
movies");
```

## Running Statements

Once constructed, the SQL statements, contained within the Statement object, can be run against the database by calling the execute method (Listing 6-2).

***Listing 6-2.*** Executing the SQL statements contained within a Statement object

```
Publisher<? extends Result> publisher = statement.execute();
```

Depending on the nature of the SQL command or commands that have been executed, the resulting Publisher object may return one or many Result objects.

### Sneak Peek

A Result object is an implementation of the Result interface provided by the R2DBC specification (Listing 6-3).

***Listing 6-3.*** The Result interface

```
public interface Result {
    Publisher<Integer> getRowsUpdated();
    <T> Publisher<T> map(BiFunction<Row, RowMetadata, ? extends T>
    mappingFunction);
}
```

The Result object is responsible for providing two results types:

- The number of records, or rows, updated as a result of the executed SQL statements via the getRowsUpdated method

- A result set organized in a tabular fashion via the map method

The Result interface, its characteristics, and its uses are examined in greater detail later in this book.

# Dynamic Input

Of course, it's often the case that SQL statements need to include information, like filters, to target specific data. You may also want to reuse particular SQL statements by simply swapping values dynamically (Listing 6-4).

*Listing 6-4.* Appending a value directly to the SQL statement string

```
String artist = "Johnny Data";
Statement statement = connection.createStatement("SELECT title FROM songs
WHERE artist = '" + artist + "'");
```

Unfortunately, doing something like what I've done in the preceding code can lead to unintended consequences such as opening up your statements to vulnerabilities like SQL injection.

---

**Note**   SQL injection is a code injection technique used to attack data-driven applications, in which malicious statements are inserted into an entry field for execution.

---

Luckily, the R2DBC specification allows driver implementations the ability to take advantage of parameterization, or the process of adding parameters to SQL statements, by using vendor-specific *bind markers* within a SQL string assigned to a Statement object. Bind markers are special characters that are used to denote variables within a query string. Bind variables can be bound by a marker's index or by name.

**Caution**    All bind variables indicated within a SQL statement must be supplied and of the correct type, or an error will occur when attempting to execute the statement.

## Creating Parameterized Statements

The process of creating a parameterized Statement object is done the same way as creating non-parameterized statements, through the createStatement method on the Connection object (Listings 6-5, 6-6, and 6-7).

***Listing 6-5.*** Creating a named parameterized statement for MariaDB or MySQL

```
Statement statement = connection.createStatement("SELECT title FROM songs
WHERE artist = :artist");
```

***Listing 6-6.*** Creating a named parameterized statement for Microsoft SQL Server

```
Statement statement = connection.createStatement("SELECT title FROM songs
WHERE artist = @PO");
```

***Listing 6-7.*** Creating a named parameterized statement for PostgreSQL

```
Statement statement = connection.createStatement("SELECT title FROM songs
WHERE artist = $1");
```

Because the bind markers are identified within Statement objects, parameterized statements may be cached for reuse.

**Note**    Caching parameterized, or prepared, statements is a method that is used to execute the same or similar database statements repeatedly with high efficiency.

# Binding Parameters

Once you've created a parameterized statement, you will need to assign values to the defined parameters. The Statement interface defines two methods to provide parameter values for bind marker substitution, bind and bindNull.

Statement binding methods accept two arguments:

1. Either an ordinal, zero-based, position or a named placeholder parameter

2. The value to be assigned to the parameter

***Listing 6-8.*** Binding parameters to a Statement object using placeholders

```
Statement statement = connection.createStatement("SELECT title FROM songs
WHERE title = $1 and artist = $2");
statement.bind("$1", "No Errors");
statement.bind("$2", "Lil Data");
```

***Listing 6-9.*** Binding parameters to a Statement object by index

```
Statement statement = connection.createStatement("SELECT title FROM songs
WHERE title = $1 and artist = $2");
statement.bind(0, "No Errors");
statement.bind(1, "Lil Data");
```

Each bind marker within the Statement object must have an associated value before the statement can be run. The execute method, within the Statement object, is responsible for validating parameterized statements. If a bind marker is missing, an IllegalStateException will be thrown.

# Batching Statements

The Statement object also supports binding of multiple parameters, organized as batched commands that can be executed on an underlying database.

---

**Note**   A batch is a set of SQL statements submitted together and executed as a group, one after the other.

---

Batches can be created by first providing the parameters, through the use of the bind method, and then using the add method. From there, the next set of parameter bindings can be provided.

***Listing 6-10.*** Creating and running a Statement batch

```
Statement statement = connection.createStatement("INSERT INTO songs (title,
artist) VALUES ($1, $2)");
statement.bind(0, "Give me that SQL").bind(1, "Johnny Data").add();
statement.bind(0, "Doo-Doo-Data").bind(1, "Susie SQL").add();
statement.bind(0, "Relationship woes").bind(1, "Column Crew");
Publisher<? extends Result> publisher = statement.execute();
```

The driver implementation is responsible for creating the corresponding SQL statements from the Statement batch.

***Listing 6-11.*** An example set of MariaDB-based SQL statements

```
INSERT INTO songs (title, artist) VALUES ('Give me that SQL', 'Johnny
Data'); INSERT INTO songs (title, artist) VALUES ('Doo-Doo-Data', 'Susie
SQL');
```

Ultimately, a batch run emits one or many Result objects, which depends on how the implementation prepares and executes Statement batches.

## Using Null Values

NULL values are handled separately using a method called bindNull, which takes two parameters:

1. Either an ordinal, zero-based, position or a named placeholder parameter

2. The *nullable* value type of the parameter

***Listing 6-12.*** Binding a NULL value parameter by index

```
statement.bindNull(0, String.class);
```

# Auto-generated Values

Oftentimes we need to take advantage of data, usually identifiers, within our tables that have been automatically generated by the database management system. Many database systems perform automatic value generation when a row is inserted that may or may not be unique.

Because of the differences in how database systems go about creating and accessing auto-generated values, rather than dictating an implementation, the R2DBC specification provides a method called `returnGeneratedValues` on the `Statement` interface that vendor-specific drivers can provide implementations for. The method accepts a variable-argument parameter used to pinpoint the column names that contain auto-generated values (Listing 6-13).

***Listing 6-13.*** Creating a statement with the returnGeneratedValues method

```
Statement statement = connection.createStatement("INSERT INTO songs (title,
artist) VALUES ('Primary Key to My Heart', 'Tina Tables')").returnGenerated
Values("id");
```

The emitted `Result` object contains columns, available within the `Row` object, for each of the automatically generated values requested. The `Row` interface used for `Row` object implementation will be described in greater detail later in this book.

***Listing 6-14.*** Retrieving auto-generated values

```
Publisher<? extends Result> publisher = statement.execute();
publisher.map((row, metadata) -> row.get("id"));
```

# Performance Hints

The `Statement` interface provides a method called `fetchSize` that can be used to provide back pressure hints to a R2DBC driver. From a high level, the method's role is to apply a fetch size SQL hint to each query produced by the statement.

**Note**    A *hint* is an addition to the SQL standard that instructs the database engine on how to execute the query. For example, a hint may tell the engine to use or not to use an index.

More specifically, the `fetchSize` method's purpose is to retrieve a fixed number of rows when fetching results from a query instead deriving fetch size from back pressure. If called multiple times, only the fetch size configured in the final invocation will be applied. If the value specified is zero, then the hint is ignored. The default implementation of the method is a no-op, and the default value is zero.

Back pressure hints can be used by drivers to derive an appropriate fetch size. To optimize for performance, it can be useful to provide hints to the driver on a per-statement basis to avoid unwanted interference of back pressure hint propagation.

**Caution**    Back pressure should be considered a utility for flow control and not to limit the result size. Result size limitations should be part of the query statement.

Hints provided to the driver through the `Statement` interface may be ignored by the driver if they are not appropriate or supported by the underlying database.

# Summary

Providing a database with information in order to retrieve some sort of results or feedback is one of the most important tasks, if not the most important task, involved in creating a database-backed application.

In this chapter, we learned about the functionality and guidelines dictated by the R2DBC specification that make communicating SQL statements to the underlying databases possible. We also examined the options available for providing parameterized statements to improve the security and efficiency of our database communications.

# CHAPTER 7

# Handling Results

Connecting to a database and executing SQL statements is great, but at the end of the day, if we can't obtain data from the database, what's the point? In this chapter, we're going to take a look at how the R2DBC specification organizes and exposes functionality that makes retrieving data from a database a piece of cake.

You'll start by gaining an understanding of the fundamental steps involved in obtaining data. Then we'll dive deeper into the object landscape to examine the plethora of functionality that enables truly reactive access to relationally stored data.

## The Fundamentals

As briefly touched upon in Chapter 6, a `Result` object is created and obtained as the result of running a SQL statement within a `Statement` object. The `Statement` object's execute method returns a `Publisher` that *emits* `Result` objects as the result of running the underlying SQL statement (Listing 7-1).

***Listing 7-1.*** Obtaining a result via SQL statement execution.

```
Statement statement = connection.createStatement("SELECT album_id, title,
artist FROM songs");
Publisher<? extends Result> results = statement.execute();
```

---

**Tip**   Check out Chapter 13 to see `Statement` object implementations of the methods we'll be examining in this chapter.

---

Result objects are objects that allow consumption of two result types (Figure 7-1):

- The number of rows that have been updated as a result of the executed SQL statements

© Robert Hedgpeth 2021
R. Hedgpeth, *R2DBC Revealed*, https://doi.org/10.1007/978-1-4842-6989-3_7

- A set of results, organized in a tabular fashion, retrieved by the SQL statements

**Result object**

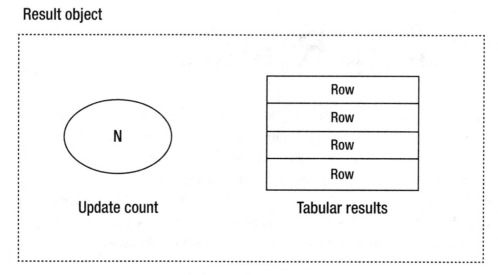

**Figure 7-1.** *The two types of results available within a R2DBC Result object, number of records updated and tabular result set*

The R2DBC specification provides an interface called `Result` that driver implementations use to create a `Result` object implementation (Listing 7-2).

*Listing 7-2.* The Result interface.

```
import org.reactivestreams.Publisher;
import java.util.function.BiFunction;
public interface Result {
    Publisher<Integer> getRowsUpdated();
    <T> Publisher<T> map(BiFunction<Row, RowMetadata, ? extends T>
    mappingFunction);
}
```

# Consuming Results

The process of obtaining results involves handling emission of Row objects, where results move forward from the first Row to the last one. After emitting the last row, a Result object gets invalidated, and rows from the same Result object can no longer be consumed.

Rows contained in the result depend on how the underlying database materializes the results. That is, it contains the rows that satisfy the query either at the time the query is run or as the rows are retrieved.

---

**Note**    The Row object will be examined in more detail later in this chapter.

---

# Cursors

An R2DBC driver can obtain a Result either directly or by using cursors, which are control structures that enable traversal over records within a database (Figure 7-2).

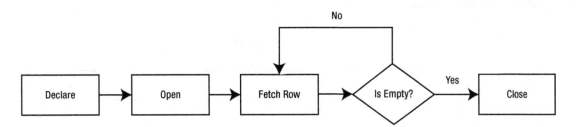

***Figure 7-2.***  *The workflow of a cursor*

By consuming Row objects, an R2DBC driver is responsible for advancing the cursor position. If a subscription to the tabular results is canceled, the cursor read process will be stopped, and any resources associated with the Result object will be released.

# Update Count

Through use of the getRowsUpdated method, the Result object reports the number of rows affected for SQL statements, such as updates for SQL Data Manipulation Language (DML) statements.

> **Note**   The SQL Data Manipulation Language is a sublanguage SQL that consists of operations that involve adding, deleting, or modifying data in a database.

***Listing 7-3.*** Consuming a Result update count.

```
Publisher<Integer> rowsUpdated = result.getRowsUpdated();
```

After emitting the update count, a `Result` object gets invalidated, and rows from the same `Result` object can no longer be consumed. The update count can be empty for statements that do not modify rows.

# Rows and Columns

As I pointed out before, the `Result` interface provides a map method that is used to retrieve values from `Row` objects. Rows, which represent single rows of tabular results, however, are only one piece of the puzzle. As you know, tables are made of two types of entities: rows and columns (Figure 7-3).

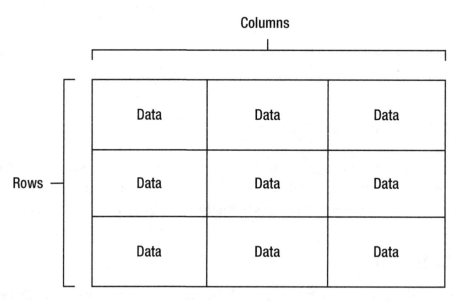

***Figure 7-3.*** *Tabular data consists of both rows and columns*

Based on this, data is retrieved from the Row object by targeting a contained column field (Figure 7-4).

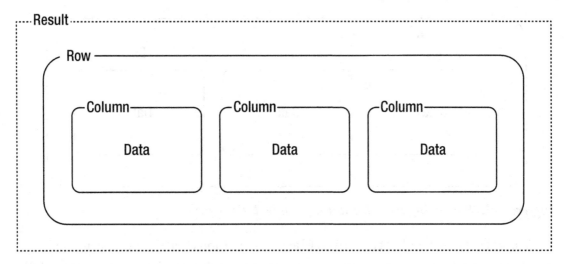

***Figure 7-4.*** *The R2DBC result hierarchy*

## Row Anatomy

The Row interface, which is used by implementing drivers to provide a Row object, contains four methods, all named get:

- Object get(int)

- Object get(String)

- <T> T get(int, Class<T>)

- <T> T get(String, Class<T>)

The get(int) and get(int, Class<T>) methods both accept an integer value, starting at 0, which is used to find and return the value of a column at a specified index (Figure 7-5).

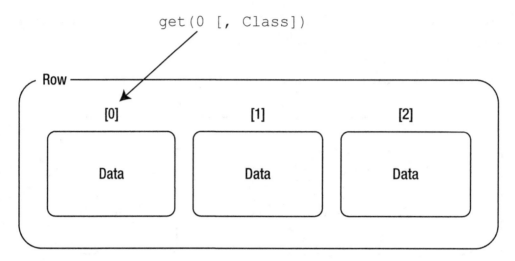

***Figure 7-5.*** *Retrieving data from a Row object using an index*

The get(String) and get(String, Class<T>) methods both accept a string value, which is used to find and return the value of a column with a specified name (Figure 7-6).

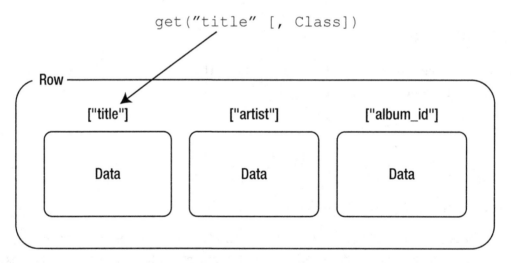

***Figure 7-6.*** *Retrieving data from a Row object using a column name*

Column names used as input to the get method are case insensitive and do not necessarily reflect the column names as they are in the underlying tables but, rather, how columns are represented or *aliased* in the result.

**Note**    Aliases are used to give a database table, or a column in a table, a temporary name. Aliases are often used to make column names more readable or descriptive. An alias only exists for the duration of the query it's contained in.

# Retrieving Values

A Row is only valid during the mapping function callback and is invalid outside of the mapping function callback. Thus, Row objects must be entirely consumed by the *mapping* function.

**Tip**    The *mapping* function refers to the map method in the Result object as indicated previously in this chapter.

## Generic Objects

Using the get method without specifying a target type will return a suitable value representation (Listings 7-4 and 7-5).

*Listing 7-4.* Creating and consuming a Row object using an index.

```
Publisher<Object> values = result.map((row, rowMetadata) -> row.get(0));
```

*Listing 7-5.* Creating and consuming a Row object using a column name.

```
Publisher<Object> values = result.map((row, rowMetadata) -> row.
get("title"));
```

## Specifying Types

Including a type as an argument within the get method prompts the R2DBC driver to attempt to convert the value retrieved from the Row object into the specified type.

***Listing 7-6.*** Creating and consuming a Row object with type conversion using an index.

```
Publisher<String> values = result.map((row, rowMetadata) -> row.get(0,
String.class));
```

***Listing 7-7.*** Creating and consuming a Row object with type conversion using a column name.

```
Publisher<String> titles = result.map((row, rowMetadata) -> row.
get("title", String.class));
```

## Multiple Columns

You can specify and consume multiple columns from a Row object.

***Listing 7-8.*** Consuming multiple columns from a row using column names.

```
Publisher<Song> values = result.map((row, rowMetadata) -> {
    String title = row.get("title", String.class);
    String artist = row.get("artist", String.class);
    Integer albumId = row.get("album_id", Integer.class);

    return new Song(title, artist, albumId);
});
```

# Summary

In this chapter, we learned about the hierarchy of objects available within drivers as defined by the R2DBC specification. We learned how the `Statement` object is able to take advantage of reactive programming methodologies to provide results of SQL statement execution.

Furthermore, we dove deeper into the anatomy of the `Result` object to gain a better understanding of the capabilities for retrieving data. On top of learning about the ability to retrieve the number of records updated by SQL statements, we also took a closer look at how cursors and data mapping make it possible to access tabularly stored data within R2DBC object implementations.

# CHAPTER 8

# Result Metadata

In the previous chapter, you learned that R2DBC makes it incredibly easy for you to gain access to and consume results returned from executed SQL statements. But in order to fully utilize results returned from a database, it's often just as important to understand information about the data being returned.

Diving a little deeper, in this chapter, we're going to take a look at *how* the R2DBC specification makes it possible to not only retrieve and consume SQL results but also gain insight on the technical information of the schema itself through the use of *metadata*.

Metadata can be extremely useful in the hands of developers for a variety of reasons; and, because of this, the ability to access it through an R2DBC driver is paramount.

## Data About Data

However, before you can start to understand how to use metadata, it's important that you understand what it is. Put simply, metadata is data that provides data about other data. For relational databases, this means that metadata provides the basic and relevant information about tabular data, or the tables and the part of the tables therein.

The R2DBC specification provides two interfaces for accessing metadata for statement results, which can be used by libraries and applications to determine the properties of a *row* and its *columns*.

## Row Metadata

The first interface, RowMetadata (Listing 8-1), is used to determine the properties of, you guessed it, a row. The interface accomplishes this by exposing ColumnMetadata for each column in the result.

© Robert Hedgpeth 2021
R. Hedgpeth, *R2DBC Revealed*, https://doi.org/10.1007/978-1-4842-6989-3_8

***Listing 8-1.*** The RowMetadata interface

```
import java.util.Collection;
import java.util.NoSuchElementException;

public interface RowMetadata {
    ColumnMetadata getColumnMetadata(int index);
    ColumnMetadata getColumnMetadata(String name);
    Iterable<? extends ColumnMetadata> getColumnMetadatas();
    Collection<String> getColumnNames();
}
```

Using the getColumnMetadata methods, data about individual columns can be retrieved using an index or a column name. The RowMetadata object also exposes the ability to access the entire collection of column data through the getColumnMetadatas method and a collection of column names through the getColumnNames method.

## Column Metadata

Column metadata is typically a by-product of statement execution, and the amount of information is dependent on the driver and underlying database vendor. Because metadata retrieval can require additional lookups, through the use of internal queries, to provide a complete set of metadata, it's possible that a database's workflow conflicts with the reactive streaming nature of R2DBC.

As a result, the ColumnMetadata interface (Listing 8-2) declares two sets of methods: methods that are required to be implemented and methods that are optional to be implemented by drivers.

***Listing 8-2.*** The ColumnMetadata interface

```
public interface ColumnMetadata {

    String getName();

    @Nullable
    default Class<?> getJavaType() {
        return null;
    }
```

```
@Nullable
default Object getNativeTypeMetadata() {
    return null;
}

default Nullability getNullability() {
    return Nullability.UNKNOWN;
}

@Nullable
default Integer getPrecision() {
    return null;
}

@Nullable
default Integer getScale() {
    return null;
}

}
```

## Required Methods

Column metadata is optionally available as a by-product of statement execution and is supplied on a "best-effort" basis. The only method that is required to be implemented by drivers is getName, which returns the name of the column. The name does not necessarily reflect the column name as how it is in the underlying table but rather how the column is represented, including aliases, in the result.

## Optional Methods

Every other method within the ColumnMetadata is optional. However, according to the R2DBC documentation, it's suggested that drivers implement as many as possible, but support will vary driver to driver based on the capabilities of the underlying database.

## getJavaType

The getJavaType method returns the primary Java type of the column value. The type returned is considered to be the native representation that is used to exchange values with the least amount of precision lost.

The R2DBC documentation recommends that drivers *should* implement getJavaType in order to return an actual type and refrain from returning an Object type. The response time of getJavaType will vary depending on the type returned.

## getNativeTypeMetadata

The getNativeTypeMetadata method returns the native type descriptor, as type Object, that, potentially, exposes more metadata. The R2DBC documentation recommends that getNativeTypeMetadata be implemented *only* if a driver is able to provide a driver-specific type metadata object that exposes any additional information.

## getNullability

The getNullability method returns the nullability, via the Nullabilty enumeration (Listing 8-3), of the column values.

***Listing 8-3.*** The Nullability enumeration

```
public enum Nullability {
    NULLABLE,
    NON_NULL,
    UNKNOWN
}
```

The default value returned by the getNullability method is Nullability.UNKNOWN.

## getPrecision

The getPrecision method returns the precision of the column. The precision value that is returned depends on the underlying type of the column.

For instance

- *Numeric data* returns the maximum precision value.

- *Character data* returns the length of characters.

– *DateTime data* returns the length, in bytes, required to represent the value, assuming the maximum allowed precision of the fractional seconds component.

### getScale

The getScale method returns the scale of the column, meaning the number of digits *to the right* of the decimal point for numeric data.

# Retrieving Metadata

Obtaining the R2DBC metadata objects requires us to think back to the information we learned in Chapter 7 on results. Remember that the Result object exposes a method called map, which functions to map the rows that are returned within the Result.

## Obtaining a RowMetadata Object

A RowMetadata object is created during the process of using Result.map(…) to consume the tabular results. For each Row that is created, a RowMetadata object is also created. From that, as indicated in Listing 8-4, you are then able to use the RowMetadata object to obtain column metadata.

***Listing 8-4.*** Using a RowMetadata object to access and retrieve column metadata

```
// result is a Result object
result.map(new BiFunction<Row, RowMetadata, Object>() {

    @Override
    public Object apply(Row row, RowMetadata rowMetadata) {
        ColumnMetadata my_column = rowMetadata.getColumnMetadata(
        "column_name");
        Nullability nullability = my_column.getNullability();
    }

});
```

## Accessing ColumnMetadata

Once you've successfully obtained a RowMetadata object from a Result, you are able to access the implemented methods available within the ColumnMetadata object.

*Listing 8-5.* Retrieving column information through the ColumnMetadata object

```
// row is a RowMetadata object
row.getColumnMetadatas().forEach(columnMetadata -> {
    String name = columnMetadata.getName();
    Integer precision = columnMetadata.getPrecision();
    Integer scale = columnMetadata.getScale();
});
```

# Summary

Applications can use information that describes data and the way it's stored in a variety of ways. In fact, retrieving and consuming metadata can be a very powerful tool in your toolbelt.

In this chapter, we learned that the R2DBC specification uses the Result object to expose metadata through the RowMetadata and ColumnMetadata interfaces. Taking a step further, and depending on the driver's vendor, we examined the possible methods available for extracting crucial information about the columns coinciding with our results.

# CHAPTER 9

# Mapping Data Types

In computer science, a data type is a data storage format that can contain a specific type of range of values. Basically, when data is stored, each unit must be assigned to a specific type in order to be universally useful.

Data type characteristics and requirements can vary drastically between programming languages. And, of course, the Structured Query Language (SQL) is no exception to this. In this chapter, we'll be examining how the R2DBC specification provides support for common SQL data types, how they are mapped to the Java programming language, and how they can be used within applications.

## Data Type Differences

SQL data types define the types of values that can be stored in a table column. There are many data types available, as seen in Figure 9-1.

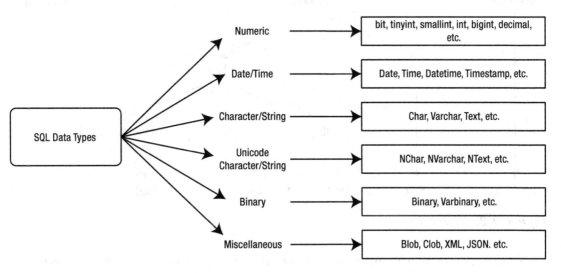

*Figure 9-1. SQL data types*

© Robert Hedgpeth 2021
R. Hedgpeth, *R2DBC Revealed*, https://doi.org/10.1007/978-1-4842-6989-3_9

However, not all of the data types listed in the preceding diagram are supported by every relational database vendor, and some vendors even provide additional data types. And even though some vendors may align on particular data types that are supported, it is likely they have different size limitations per type.

As you know, applications aren't built with SQL alone. Remember that R2DBC drivers are meant to provide support for JVM languages, which can be used to build applications, to communicate with relational databases in a reactive manner. The Java programming language, for example, contains its own data types that are divided into two main groups: primitive and non-primitive (Figure 9-2).

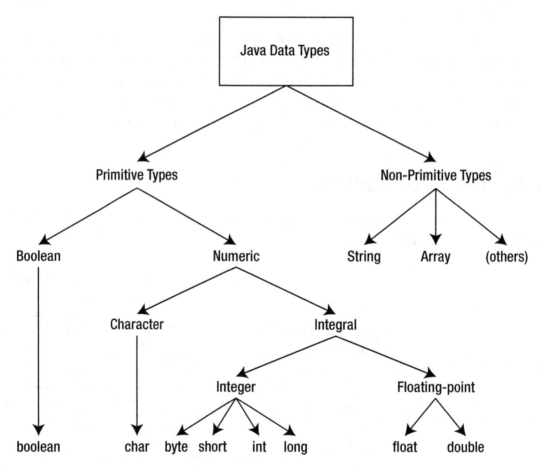

**Figure 9-2.** *Java data types*

This creates a scenario that in order to be able to use SQL data types, regardless of vendor, with a programming language like Java or any other application development language, a process of mapping, or data translation, must be done.

Luckily, the R2DBC specification provides application access to the data types that are defined within SQL. In fact, R2DBC is not limited only to SQL types as it is type agnostic, which we'll dive into later in this chapter.

---

**Tip**   According to the R2DBC specification documentation, if a data source does not support a data type described within this chapter, a driver for that data source is not required to implement the methods and interfaces associated with that data type.

---

# Mapping Simple Data Types

The R2DBC specification documentation indicates a list of data types that can be used as a guideline for implementing drivers. R2DBC drivers should use modern data types and type descriptors to exchange data with applications.

# Character Types

The Character and varying character data types accept character strings or a linear sequence of characters of a fixed or variable length, respectively (Table 9-1).

***Table 9-1.***  *SQL/Java type mapping for character types*

| SQL Type | Java Type | Description |
| --- | --- | --- |
| Character (CHAR) | java.lang.String | Character string, fixed length. |
| Character Varying (VARCHAR) | java.lang.String | Variable-length character string, maximum length fixed. |
| National Character (NCHAR) | java.lang.String | Like Character but holds standardized multibyte or Unicode characters. |
| National Varying Character (NVARCHAR) | java.lang.String | Like Character Varying but holds standardized multibyte or Unicode characters. |

(*continued*)

**Table 9-1.**  (*continued*)

| SQL Type | Java Type | Description |
|---|---|---|
| Character Large Object (CLOB) | java.lang.String, io.r2dbc.spi.Clob | A CLOB is a collection of character data in a database management system. |
| National Character Large Object (NLOB) | java.lang.String, io.r2dbc.spi.Clob | Like CLOB but holds standardized multibyte characters or Unicode characters. |

# Boolean Types

The Boolean data type supports the storage of two values: TRUE and FALSE.

**Table 9-2.**  *SQL/Java type mapping for Boolean types*

| SQL Type | Java Type | Description |
|---|---|---|
| BOOLEAN | java.lang.Boolean | A value that represents a Boolean (true/false) state. |

**Note**    Though this is a fairly straightforward type, it's important to note that not all database management systems contain an explicit Boolean type. For example, MySQL and MariaDB use `TINYINT(1)`, which specifies an `INTEGER` of length 1 to contain the value of either 1, for True, or 0, for False.

# Binary Types

Relational databases use binary data types to store binary data, which is used for things like images, text files, audio files, and so on.

*Table 9-3.  SQL/Java type mapping for binary types*

| SQL Type | Java Type | Description |
|---|---|---|
| BINARY | java.nio.ByteBuffer | Binary data, fixed length. |
| Binary Varying (VARBINARY) | java.nio.ByteBuffer | A variable-length character string, the maximum length of which is used. |
| Binary Large Object (BLOB) | java.nio.ByteBuffer, io.r2dbc.spi.Blob | A BLOB is a collection of binary data in a database management system. |

# Numeric Types

Numbers can be presented in many different ways. For example, they can be whole, fractional, positive, or negative. As a result, relational databases provide a variety of data types to accommodate such requirements.

*Table 9-4.  SQL/Java type mapping for numeric types*

| SQL Type | Java Type | Description |
|---|---|---|
| INTEGER | java.lang.Integer | Represents an integer. The minimum and maximum values depend on the database management system (typically 4-byte precision). |
| TINYINT | java.lang.Byte | Like INTEGER but it may hold a smaller range of values, depending on the database management system (typically 1-byte precision). |
| SMALLINT | java.lang.Short | Like INTEGER but it might hold a smaller range of values, depending on the database management system (typically 1- or 2-byte precision). |
| BIGINT | java.lang.Long | Like INTEGER but it might hold a larger range of values, depending on the database management system (typically 8-byte precision). |
| DECIMAL(p,s) NUMERIC(p,s) | java.math. BigDecimal | Fixed precision and scale number with precision (p) and scale (s). A number that can represent a decimal point value. |

*(continued)*

**Table 9-4.** (*continued*)

| SQL Type | Java Type | Description |
|---|---|---|
| FLOAT(p) | java.lang.Double, java.lang.Float | Represents an approximate numerical with mantissa precision (p). Databases that use IEEE representation can map values to either 32-bit or 64-bit floating-point types depending on the precision parameter (p). |
| REAL | java.lang.Float | Like FLOAT but the database management system defines the precision. |
| DOUBLE PRECISION | java.lang.Double | Like FLOAT but the database management system defines precision. |

**Note**    In the preceding table, *p* stands for *precision* and *s* for *scale*.

# DateTime Types

Dates and times are stored using types that accommodate each and the combination of the two. Database management systems also provide functionality for managing time zones.

**Table 9-5.**  *SQL/Java type mapping for DateTime types.*

| SQL Type | Java Type | Description |
|---|---|---|
| DATE | java.time.LocalDate | Represents a date without specifying a time part and without a time zone. |
| TIME | java.time.LocalTime | Represents a time without a date part and without a time zone. |
| TIME WITH TIME ZONE | java.time.OffsetTime | Represents a time with a time zone offset. |
| TIMESTAMP | java.time.LocalDateTime | Represents a date and time without a time zone. |
| TIMESTAMP WITH TIME ZONE | java.time.OffsetDateTime | Represents a date and time with a time zone offset. |

## Collection Types

Some database vendors provide types for collection data like arrays and multisets.

***Table 9-6.*** *SQL/Java type mapping for collection types.*

| SQL Type | Java Type | Description |
|---|---|---|
| COLLECTION (ARRAY, MULTISET) | Array variant of the corresponding Java type (e.g., Integer[] for INTEGER ARRAY) | Represents a collection of items with a base type. |

# Mapping Advanced Data Types

So far in this chapter, we've examined simple data types that are supported by the R2DBC specification. However, when working with data, the need to store extremely large amounts of data may arise.

While earlier versions of relational databases tended to handle this scenario with existing types such as VARCHAR and NVARCHAR, it quickly became apparent that more advanced data types were necessary.

Large Objects, or LOBs, were created to store data in such a way that optimizes space and provides a more efficient method for accessing large data. In the next section, we'll be taking a closer look at how R2DBC handles two types of LOBs: BLOBs and CLOBs.

## BLOBs and CLOBs

BLOBs, or Binary Large Objects, are a data type that stores binary data, which is different from other data types, like integers and characters, used in relational databases that store letters and numbers. Allowing the storage of binary data makes it possible for databases to contain things like images, videos, or other multimedia files.

---

**Note**   Because BLOBs are used to store objects such as photos and audio or video files, they often require significantly more space than other data types. The amount of data a BLOB can store varies depending on the database management system.

---

CLOBs, or Character Large Objects, are similar to BLOBs in that they also exist to store large amounts of data. The key difference, however, is that CLOB data is stored using text encoding methods such as ASCII and Unicode.

---

**Tip**    The key takeaway here is that you can think of BLOBs as containing large amounts of binary data, while CLOBs contain large amounts of character, or text, data.

---

Driver implementations of `Blob` or `Clob` objects may either be locator-based or fully materialized objects in the driver. According to the R2DBC specification documentation, drivers should prefer locator-based `Blob` and `Clob` implementations to reduce pressure on clients that are to materialize the results.

## Creating Objects

In Java, LOBs are backed by a `Publisher` object that emits the component type of the specific type of large object, such as `ByteBuffer` for BLOB and the Java interface type `CharSequence` for CLOB.

---

**Note**    Ultimately, CLOBs are handled as a `String` type, which implements the `CharSequence` interface.

---

The R2DBC `Blob` and `Clob` interfaces provide factory methods for creating implementations that can be used by the `Statement` object (Listing 9-1).

*Listing 9-1.* Blob factory method used to provide a usable implementation.

```
static Blob from(Publisher<ByteBuffer> p) {
    Assert.requireNonNull(p, "Publisher must not be null");
    DefaultLob<ByteBuffer> lob = new DefaultLob<>(p);
    return new Blob() {
        @Override
        public Publisher<ByteBuffer> stream() {
            return lob.stream();
        }
```

```
    @Override
    public Publisher<Void> discard() {
        return lob.discard();
    }
};
}
```

A similar method exists within the Clob interface, and, as such, the steps for creating and using Blob and Clob objects are also similar.

***Listing 9-2.*** Creating and using a Blob

```
// binaryStream is a Publisher<ByteBuffer> object
// statement is a Statement object
Blob blob = Blob.from(binaryStream);
statement.bind("image", blob);
```

***Listing 9-3.*** Creating and using a Clob

```
// characterStream is a Publisher<String> object
// statement is a Statement object
Clob clob = Clob.from(characterStream);
statement.bind("text", clob);
```

# Retrieving Objects

The BLOB and CLOB data types are treated similarly to primitive, built-in, types. In fact, the BLOB and CLOB values can be retrieved by using the get methods of a Row object.

***Listing 9-4.*** Retrieving a Blob object

```
Publisher<Blob> blob = result.map((row, rowMetadata) -> row.get("blob",
Blob.class));
```

***Listing 9-5.*** Retrieving a Clob object

```
Publisher<Clob> clob = result.map((row, rowMetadata) -> row.get("clob",
Clob.class));
```

## Consuming Objects

The Blob and Clob interfaces expose a method called stream that provides a way for clients to consume their respective content. Keeping in line with the Reactive Streams specification, content streams are used to transfer the large objects.

***Listing 9-6.*** Accessing a Blob object using the stream method

```
Publisher<ByteBuffer> binaryStream = blob.stream();
```

***Listing 9-7.*** Accessing a Clob object using the stream method

```
Publisher<CharSequence> characterStream = clob.stream();
```

It's important to note that streams can only be consumed once and the data can be called anytime during the process by executing the discard method.

## Releasing Objects

Because Blob and Clob objects remain valid during the duration of their transaction, it's possible that long-running transactions will cause the application to run out of resources. Keeping this in mind, the R2DBC specification provides implementations with a method called discard, which can be used by applications to release Blob and Clob object resources.

***Listing 9-8.*** Releasing Blob object resources

```
Publisher<Void> binaryStream = blob.discard();
binaryStream.subscribe();
```

***Listing 9-9.*** Releasing Clob object resources

```
Publisher<Void> characterStream = clob.discard();
characterStream.subscribe();
```

# Summary

Understanding data types is an important part of being able to effectively and efficiently manage information. In fact, if you think about it, classifying types of data is one of the *most* crucial concepts of relational database management systems. Without them, the enforcing principles like data integrity would be impossible.

In this chapter, we learned about the data types that R2DBC aims to support and how they can be used. We also examined more advanced data types, like BLOBs and CLOBs, and how they utilize reactive programming capabilities and can be created, consumed, and destroyed.

# CHAPTER 10

# Handling Exceptions

Imagine a scenario where you're writing an application and every time you compile and run your code everything works flawlessly. OK, you can stop laughing now. Whether you're a novice or seasoned developer, one thing is constant: exceptions occurring. While it would be nice if our code worked without problems, but for one reason or another, we're bound to encounter problems. Luckily, we have the ability to prepare our code to account for and manage exceptions.

In this chapter, we're going to take a look at types of exceptions that R2DBC defines and uses to provide information about various types of failures you may encounter.

## General Exceptions

Exceptions are thrown by an R2DBC driver for two reasons.

1.  During an interaction with the driver itself
2.  During an interaction with the underlying data source

R2DBC distinguishes between generic, or those that may occur within the driver code, and data source–specific error cases.

## IllegalArgumentException

Drivers throw `IllegalArgumentException` to indicate that a method, within an R2DBC object, has received an illegal or invalid argument. Invalid arguments include scenarios where the values may be out of bounds or an expected parameter is null.

`IllegalArgumentException` extends the `RuntimeException` class and, thus, belongs to those exceptions that can be thrown during the operation of the JVM. It is an *unchecked* exception, and thus, it does not need to be declared in a method's or a constructor's throws clause.

© Robert Hedgpeth 2021
R. Hedgpeth, *R2DBC Revealed*, https://doi.org/10.1007/978-1-4842-6989-3_10

---

**Note**   An unchecked exception is an exception that occurs at the time of execution. These are also called as *runtime exceptions*. These include programming bugs, such as logic errors or improper use of an API. Runtime exceptions are ignored at the time of compilation.

---

# IllegalStateException

IllegalStateException, which also extends RuntimeException, signals that a method has been invoked at an illegal or inappropriate time. R2DBC drivers throw IllegalStateException to indicate that a method has received an argument that is invalid in the current state or when an argument-less method is involved in a state that does not allow execution of the current state, for example, if there is an attempt to interact with an object that has already closed its connection.

# UnsupportedOperationException

Extending RuntimeException, the UnsupportedOperationException class is fairly self-explanatory. It is thrown to indicate that a requested operation is not supported. For R2DBC drivers, this means that it will be thrown when the driver does not support certain functionality, such as when a method implementation has not been provided.

# R2DBCException

The R2dbcException abstract class extends RuntimeException and functions as a root exception that is meant to be extended by all server-related exceptions within an R2DBC implementation. Drivers will throw an instance of R2dbcException when an error occurs during an interaction with a data source.

An R2dbcException object will contain the following information:

- A description of the error. Descriptions are textual, can be localized within driver implementations, and can be retrieved by invoking the getMessage method.

- A SQLState, which is retrieved as a String by invoking the getSqlState method. According to the R2DBC specification documentation, the value of the SQLState string depends on the underlying data source and will follow either the XOPEN SQLState or the SQL:2003 conventions.

- An error code, which is retrieved as an Integer by invoking the getErrorCode method. The values and meanings of the error code values are specific to the vendor implementation.

- A cause, which is returned as a Throwable that caused the R2dbcException to be thrown.

---

**Note**   The Throwable class is the superclass of all errors and exceptions in the Java language. Only objects that are instances of this class (or one of its subclasses) are thrown by the JVM or can be thrown by the Java throw statement.

---

Driver implementations are able to create R2dbcException objects through several constructors and take in variable combinations of reason, sqlState, errorCode, and cause parameters. After values have been set, R2dbcException provides getter methods for retrieving the exception details (Listing 10-1).

***Listing 10-1.***   The R2dbcException abstract class

```
package io.r2dbc.spi;

/**
 * A root exception that should be extended by all server-related
   exceptions in an implementation.
 */
public abstract class R2dbcException extends RuntimeException {

    private final int errorCode;

    private final String sqlState;

    /**
     * Creates a new {@link R2dbcException}.
     */
```

```
public R2dbcException() {
    this((String) null);
}

/**
 * Creates a new {@link R2dbcException}.
 *
 * @param reason the reason for the error.  Set as the exception's
   message and retrieved with {@link #getMessage()}.
 */
public R2dbcException(@Nullable String reason) {
    this(reason, (String) null);
}

/**
 * Creates a new {@link R2dbcException}.
 *
 * @param reason    the reason for the error.  Set as the exception's
   message and retrieved with {@link #getMessage()}.
 * @param sqlState the "SQLState" string, which follows either the
   XOPEN SQLState conventions or the SQL:2003
 *                  conventions
 */
public R2dbcException(@Nullable String reason, @Nullable String sqlState) {
    this(reason, sqlState, 0);
}

/**
 * Creates a new {@link R2dbcException}.
 *
 * @param reason    the reason for the error.  Set as the exception's
   message and retrieved with {@link #getMessage()}.
 * @param sqlState  the "SQLState" string, which follows either the
   XOPEN SQLState conventions or the SQL:2003
 *                  conventions
 * @param errorCode a vendor-specific error code representing this failure
 */
```

```java
public R2dbcException(@Nullable String reason, @Nullable String
sqlState, int errorCode) {
    this(reason, sqlState, errorCode, null);
}

/**
 * Creates a new {@link R2dbcException}.
 *
 * @param reason    the reason for the error.  Set as the exception's
   message and retrieved with {@link #getMessage()}.
 * @param sqlState  the "SQLState" string, which follows either the
   XOPEN SQLState conventions or the SQL:2003
 *                  conventions
 * @param errorCode a vendor-specific error code representing this
   failure
 * @param cause     the cause
 */
public R2dbcException(@Nullable String reason, @Nullable String
sqlState, int errorCode, @Nullable Throwable cause) {
    super(reason, cause);
    this.sqlState = sqlState;
    this.errorCode = errorCode;
}

/**
 * Creates a new {@link R2dbcException}.
 *
 * @param reason    the reason for the error.  Set as the exception's
   message and retrieved with {@link #getMessage()}.
 * @param sqlState the "SQLState" string, which follows either the
   XOPEN SQLState conventions or the SQL:2003
 *                  conventions
 * @param cause     the cause
 */
```

```java
public R2dbcException(@Nullable String reason, @Nullable String
sqlState, @Nullable Throwable cause) {
    this(reason, sqlState, 0, cause);
}

/**
 * Creates a new {@link R2dbcException}.
 *
 * @param reason the reason for the error.  Set as the exception's
   message and retrieved with {@link #getMessage()}.
 * @param cause   the cause
 */
public R2dbcException(@Nullable String reason, @Nullable Throwable
cause) {
    this(reason, null, cause);
}

/**
 * Creates a new {@link R2dbcException}.
 *
 * @param cause the cause
 */
public R2dbcException(@Nullable Throwable cause) {
    this(null, cause);
}

/**
 * Returns the vendor-specific error code.
 *
 * @return the vendor-specific error code
 */
public final int getErrorCode() {
    return errorCode;
}
```

```java
/**
 * Returns the SQLState.
 *
 * @return the SQLState
 */
@Nullable
public final String getSqlState() {
    return this.sqlState;
}

@Override
public String toString() {

    StringBuilder builder = new StringBuilder(32);
    builder.append(getClass().getName());

    if (getErrorCode() != 0 || (getSqlState() != null && !getSqlState()
        .isEmpty()) || getMessage() != null) {
        builder.append(":");
    }

    if (getErrorCode() != 0) {
        builder.append(" [").append(getErrorCode()).append("]");
    }

    if (getSqlState() != null && !getSqlState().isEmpty()) {
        builder.append(" [").append(getSqlState()).append("]");
    }

    if (getMessage() != null) {
        builder.append(" ").append(getMessage());
    }

    return builder.toString();
}
}
```

# Categorized Exceptions

The R2DBC specification aims to categorize exceptions in order to provide a consistent mapping to common error states. The R2DBC specification documentation indicates

> *Categorized exceptions provide a standardized approach for R2DBC clients and R2DBC users to translate common exceptions into an application-specific state without the need to implement SQLState-based exception translation, resulting in more portable error-handling code.*

At the highest level, R2DBC categorizes exceptions into two categories: *non-transient* and *transient*.

# Non-transient Exceptions

Non-transient exceptions are those that will fail again on retry until the underlying cause of the problem is corrected. R2DBC non-transient exceptions must extend the abstract class R2dbcNonTransientException, which is a subclass of R2dbcException.

The R2DBC specification contains four subclasses of non-transient exceptions (Table 10-1).

***Table 10-1.*** *Non-transient exception subclasses*

| Subclass | Description |
| --- | --- |
| R2dbcBadGrammarException | Thrown when the SQL statement has a problem in its syntax. |
| R2dbcDataIntegrityViolationException | Thrown when an attempt to insert or update data results in a violation of an integrity constraint. |
| R2dbcPermissionDeniedException | Thrown when the underlying resource denied a permission to access a specific element, such as a specific database table. |
| R2dbcNonTransientException | Thrown when a resource fails completely and the failure is permanent. A connection may not be considered valid if this exception is thrown. |

# Transient Exceptions

Transient exceptions are those that when retried could succeed without changing anything. R2DBC transient exceptions are thrown when a previously failed operation *might* be able to succeed if the operation is retried without any intervention in the application-level functionality. R2DBC transient exceptions must extend the abstract class `R2dbcTransientException`, which is a subclass of `R2dbcException`.

The R2DBC specification contains two subclasses of transient exceptions (Table 10-2).

***Table 10-2.*** *Transient exception subclasses*

| Subclass | Description |
| --- | --- |
| R2dbcRollbackException | Thrown when an attempt to commit a transaction resulted in an unexpected rollback due to deadlock or transaction serialization failures. |
| R2dbcTimeoutException | Thrown when the timeout specified by a database operation is exceeded. |

# Summary

When working with databases, it's inevitable that, at some point, you'll encounter errors and have to deal with exceptions that have been thrown. Regardless of your experience, exception handling is a normal part of modern application development.

In this chapter, we examined a variety of exception classes that R2DBC uses to illuminate issues that may be encountered. You gained an understanding of the general exceptions that R2DBC drivers use as well as the custom exception class hierarchy that is used to provide deeper insight into non-transient and transient exceptions.

# PART III

# Getting Started with R2DBC and MariaDB

# CHAPTER 11

# Getting Started with R2DBC

Now that you've gotten an overview of the R2DBC specification, its overall structure, and its general workflow and a glimpse into its capabilities, you're ready to jump into an implementation. Because, to this point, you've gained a solid understanding of *what* R2DBC is and *why* it's necessary, now it's time to learn *how* to use it.

In this chapter, we'll briefly examine the official R2DBC drivers and client libraries that facilitate the creation of reactive solutions using relational databases. Ultimately, we'll walk through the process of creating a new, very basic Java project that will facilitate the usage of an R2DBC driver. The project we create in this chapter will lay the foundation for the chapters to come as we pragmatically dive into the capabilities of R2DBC.

## Database Drivers

As you've learned so far, R2DBC drivers are meant to be self-contained, compiled libraries that implement the R2DBC service-provider interface (SPI). And remember that the R2DBC SPI is deliberately designed to be as small as possible while still including features critical for any relational data store. This all ensures that the SPI does not target any extensions that may be specific to a data store.

]

Even though, at the time I'm writing this, the R2DBC SPI is not officially a general audience (GA), there are still a variety of driver implementations, spanning multiple database vendors. Table 11-1 shows that there are currently seven official, open source R2DBC drivers.

© Robert Hedgpeth 2021
R. Hedgpeth, *R2DBC Revealed*, https://doi.org/10.1007/978-1-4842-6989-3_11

***Table 11-1.*** *Official R2DBC drivers*

| Driver | Target Database(s) | Source Location |
|---|---|---|
| cloud-spanner-r2dbc | Google Cloud Spanner | `https://github.com/GoogleCloudPlatform/cloud-spanner-r2dbc` |
| jasync-sql | MySQL, PostgreSQL | `https://github.com/jasync-sql/jasync-sql` |
| r2dbc-h2 | H2 | `https://github.com/r2dbc/r2dbc-h2` |
| r2dbc-mariadb | MariaDB | `https://github.com/mariadb-corporation/mariadb-connector-r2dbc` |
| r2dbc-mssql | Microsoft SQL Server | `https://github.com/r2dbc/r2dbc-mssql` |
| r2dbc-mysql | MySQL | `https://github.com/mirromutth/r2dbc-mysql` |
| r2dbc-postgres | PostgreSQL | `https://github.com/r2dbc/r2dbc-postgresql` |

**Note**   For the purposes of this book, we'll be using the MariaDB R2DBC driver. More information will be provided later on in this chapter.

# R2DBC Client Libraries

You've learned that the R2DBC specification has been intentionally created to be lightweight in an effort to provide potential driver implementations with a large amount of creative flexibility. The simplicity of the specification also exists to discourage more opinionated, user space functionality from being included within driver implementations.

Instead, according to the official documentation, R2DBC leaves the responsibility of "humane" API functionality up to client libraries:

> *The intention of the R2DBC specification is to encourage libraries to provide a "humane" API in the form of a client library.*

What that means, from an implementation standpoint, is that applications can use client libraries which then, indirectly, use each R2DBC driver to communicate reactively with the underlying data source (Figure 11-1).

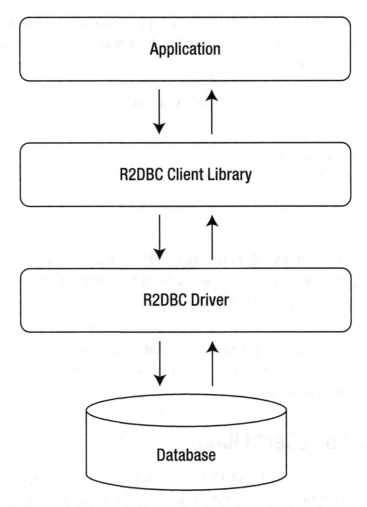

**Figure 11-1.** *R2DBC driver and client solutions function as abstractions for applications to communicate with underlying data sources*

A client library functions as an abstraction layer to help reduce the amount of boilerplate, or scaffolding, code needed to use an R2DBC driver implementation. Ultimately, if you'd like to include an R2DBC client library within your solution, there are two ways you can do so; create a new client or use an existing one.

## Creating a Client

Due to the minimalistic nature of the R2DBC SPI, the process of creating a new client is intended to be simple and straightforward. To start, client libraries just need to include the R2DBC SPI as a dependency. This can be accomplished in two ways.

The first way to include the R2DBC SPI as a dependency is by adding the group and artifact identifiers to the dependency list in a Maven-based project's pom.xml file (Listing 11-1).

***Listing 11-1.*** The R2DBC SPI dependency settings for pom.xml

```
<dependency>
    <groupId>io.r2dbc</groupId>
    <artifactId>r2dbc-spi</artifactId>
</dependency>
```

---

**Tip**   If you're unfamiliar with the process of adding dependencies to a Maven-based Java application, don't worry. We'll be diving into more detail about this process later on in this chapter!

---

The second and alternative approach is to build the R2DBC SPI directly from the source, available on GitHub, through the use of the Apache Maven Wrapper project, which is also available on GitHub.

## Use an Existing Client Library

There are currently several official R2DBC supporting clients (Table 11-2) and even more under investigation. As depicted in Figure 11-1, the existing R2DBC client libraries work by utilizing R2DBC driver implementations to handle the actual interactions with underlying data sources.

***Table 11-2.*** *Existing R2DBC client examples*

| Name | Description |
| --- | --- |
| Spring Data R2DBC | A project that enables the usage of Spring Data with the reactive development principles and repository abstraction. |
| Kotysa | A type-safe and coroutine-ready SQL engine using the Kotlin programming language. |
| jOOQ | Provides R2DBC support for the popular type-safe SQL query construction library. |

Each R2DBC client library varies in the R2DBC drivers each supports.

# Looking Ahead

There's no doubt that the decision to include an R2DBC client library is a crucial step in implementing a new truly reactive, R2DBC capable solution. However, before we can run, we need to learn how to walk. So, in this chapter, we're going to be walking through the process of setting up a project that utilizes *only* an R2DBC driver implementation. Then, in Chapters 12, 13, and 14, we'll take a closer look at exactly *how* a R2DBC driver implementation, utilizing a specific *Reactive Streams* implementation, facilitates reactive interactions with a target relational database.

Finally, in Chapter 16, after you've gained a solid understanding and level of effort necessary to create an application that uses an R2DBC driver directly, you'll learn how a specific R2DBC client library, called Spring Data R2DBC, can help drastically simplify the creation of an R2DBC capable solution.

# MariaDB and R2DBC

As previously noted, there are multiple vendors that provide R2DBC drivers, all of which provide a blend of fundamental R2DBC support and unique database capabilities. For the remainder of this book, we'll be using a single, specific R2DBC driver, provided by MariaDB, for all samples, code snippets, and walk-throughs.

---

**Note**   MariaDB is a community-developed, commercially supported fork of the MySQL relational database management system, intended to remain free and open source software under the GNU General Public License.

---

The decision to use MariaDB as the R2DBC driver and relational database of choice was not made for any particular technical reason, but rather because it provides a simple, open source, and, most importantly, free database solution to help showcase the capabilities of R2DBC.

# Introduction to MariaDB

Because I'll be using the MariaDB R2DBC driver as the example R2DBC driver implementation to demonstrate how to reactively communicate with a MariaDB database instance, in order to follow along, you'll also need to have a running MariaDB database instance. So, if you already have access to an instance of MariaDB, great! Feel free to skip ahead to the next section. However, if you're unfamiliar with MariaDB, fear not. There are a multitude of ways to start using a new, free database instance.

As I noted previously, MariaDB provides a free, open source relational database. In fact, MariaDB Server, as the free, open source version is referred to, is one of the world's most popular open source relational databases and, as such, is supported on a variety of operating systems including Windows, macOS, and Linux.

# Download and Install

The widespread availability of MariaDB not only makes installation a breeze; you also have a couple of options to choose from.

## Direct Download

Start by opening a browser and navigating to `http://mariadb.org/download`, which is supported and maintained by the MariaDB Foundation.

---

**Note**    The MariaDB Foundation is a nonprofit organization that serves as a global point of contact for collaboration for MariaDB Server.

---

From there you'll find instructions on retrieving a mariadb-server package for your operating system (OS), or, by selecting a variety of options on the page, you can indicate the package you'd like to download (Figure 11-2).

## Download MariaDB Server

MariaDB Server is one of the world's most popular open source relational databases and is available in the standard repositories of all major Linux distributions. Look for the package mariadb-server using the package manager of your operating system. Alternatively you can use the following resources:

**MariaDB Server Version**

| MariaDB Server 10.5.8 | ▾ |
| --- | --- |

Display older releases: ☐

**Operating System**

| Windows | ▾ |
| --- | --- |

**Architecture**

| x86_64 | ▾ |
| --- | --- |

**Package Type**

| MSI Package | ▾ |
| --- | --- |

| Download | Mirror | |
| --- | --- | --- |
| | Accretive Networks | ▾ |

*Figure 11-2.* *Specifying the MariaDB Server package to download*

# Docker Hub Download

The previous section provides an excellent option for downloading and installing MariaDB if you're using Windows or Linux or are interested in building MariaDB Server from the source code. But what if you're using macOS as your OS? Fear not! Another way to access MariaDB is through the use of a *container*, more specifically, in this case, a Docker container.

---

**Note**    A container is a standard unit of software that packages code and all of its dependencies so that an application can run reliably from one computing environment to another.

---

Start by navigating to `www.docker.com/get-started`. There you'll find more information on the requirements for downloading, installing, and running the software capable of facilitating Docker containers for your environment.

From there you can access the latest MariaDB Server Docker container, as well as instructions on how to download, install, and run, at `https://hub.docker.com/r/mariadb/server`, which is an official MariaDB Community Server Docker image provided by MariaDB Corporation.

---

**Note**   MariaDB Corporation is a for-profit company that provides enterprise-level MariaDB products and services. Along with the development of MariaDB Enterprise Platform, MariaDB Corporation also contributes to the open source, community version of MariaDB Server.

---

Access and Prepare

Once you've downloaded and installed a MariaDB instance, you should confirm that you have the ability to access it. This is typically done through the use of a *database client*. While there are a variety of database clients to choose from, the download and installation of MariaDB Server also includes a client that you can access through the terminal.

Simply open a terminal window and execute the command, indicated in Listing 11-2, to connect to your MariaDB instance.

***Listing 11-2.*** Connecting to a local MariaDB Server instance

```
mariadb --host 127.0.0.1 --port 3306 --user root
```

---

**Note**   The connection values indicated in Listing 11-2 assume that you've installed a MariaDB Server instance on your local machine using the default settings.

---

Alternatively, because of the default setting, you can also connect to a local MariaDB Server instance by simply using the command in Listing 11-3.

***Listing 11-3.*** Connecting to a local MariaDB Server instance using the default connection configuration

```
mariadb
```

Once you've successfully connected to MariaDB Server, you can add a new user named `app_user` by executing the SQL in Listing 11-4.

*Listing 11-4.* Creating a new MariaDB database instance user and password

```
CREATE USER 'app_user'@'%' IDENTIFIED BY 'Password123!';
GRANT ALL PRIVILEGES ON *.* TO 'app_user'@'%' WITH GRANT OPTION;
```

---

**Note**   To keep everything consistent going forward, I'll be using the `app_user` user and `Password123!` password settings for all subsequent credential-related examples.

---

# Using R2DBC

Having established access to a relational database, we've reached the point where we can use an R2DBC driver within a Java application. In fact, for the remainder of this chapter, we'll be walking through the steps of creating and running a new Java application that includes the MariaDB R2DBC driver as a dependency.

# Requirements

Before you can develop, build, and run Java applications, you'll need to make sure your system fulfills the necessary requirements to do so. The following subsections describe some needed tasks that you should perform before going on with the book.

## Install the Java Development Kit

First is to install the Java Development Kit (JDK), which is a full-featured software developer kit (SDK) that must be installed to be able to develop and run Java applications. The JDK is platform dependent, and as such the requirements for download and installation vary depending on the target platform.

For more information on how to download and install the latest release of the JDK, you can visit www.oracle.com/java/technologies/javase-downloads.html.

## Install Apache Maven

Next, you should install Apache Maven. Build management is an extremely crucial aspect of higher-order software language compilation. Apache Maven is a very popular build automation and management tool primarily used for Java. In fact, it's the most popular tool of its kind for Java.

It's for this reason, among others, that we'll be using Apache Maven as the build management tool for the R2DBC application samples going forward. For more information on Apache Maven, including how to download and install it, please visit `http://maven.apache.org`.

# Apache Maven Basics

We've reached the point where we're ready to create a new Java application to start working with an R2DBC driver to get a first-hand look at its capabilities! As you may already be aware, there are several mechanisms available you can use to create new Java projects.

In fact, if you already have experience developing Java applications, it's likely that you even have a personal preference of how to create a new application or project. Whether it be by executing commands manually within a terminal, using a specific integrated development environment (IDE), or possibly even project generation websites, there are no shortage of options.

## Create a New Project

In an effort to keep things simple and uniform, we will start by utilizing the Apache Maven software configuration management (SCM) client, a simple command-line tool, to create a new Java project.

First, choose a location within your system where you'd like to store your new project. Then, as indicated in Listing 11-5, using the Maven client, execute the following command which specifies the group, via -DgroupId; artifact, via -DartifactId; and a few other boilerplate arguments to create a new Java project.

*Listing 11-5.* The Apache Maven SCM command to create a new project

```
mvn archetype:generate -DgroupId=com.example -DartifactId=r2dbc-demo
-DarchetypeArtifactId=maven-archetype-quickstart -DarchetypeVersion=1.4
-DinteractiveMode=false
```

---

**Tip**   Using the Maven client to create a new project is just one possible approach for creating new Java projects. Ultimately, it's not important *how* you create a new Java project, just that you create a new one.

---

The -DarchetypeArtifactId=maven-archetype-quickstart argument and value is used to specify the generation of a sample Maven project (Figure 11-3).

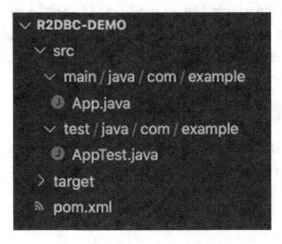

*Figure 11-3.* *Sample Maven project structure*

But now that we've used the Maven client to create a new Java project, *what* makes a Java project Maven-ready?

Ultimately, Maven projects are defined with an XML named *pom.xml*, which contains the project's name version and, most importantly, a consistent, uniform way to identify dependencies of external libraries.

## Add Dependencies

Dependencies are defined inside of the pom.xml within the dependencies node. Adding dependencies to the project involves modifying the pom.xml file.

Using a text or code editor of your choice, open the pom.xml file which is located within the root folder of the newly created project. Navigate to the dependencies node, and add a new dependency for the MariaDB R2DBC driver version 1.0.0., as indicated by the snippet in Listing 11-6.

***Listing 11-6.*** MariaDB R2DBC driver dependency

```
<dependency>
     <groupId>org.mariadb</groupId>
     <artifactId>r2dbc-mariadb</artifactId>
     <version>1.0.0</version>
</dependency>
```

---

**Note**    Maven uses the values, like groupId, artifactId, and version, contained within the dependencies node to search for internal or external libraries to add to the project.

---

## Build the Project

After adding the MariaDB R2DBC driver dependency to the project, it's the perfect time to build the project to confirm that everything has been configured correctly.

First, open a terminal window, navigate to the directory containing the pom.xml file, and execute the command shown in Listing 11-7.

***Listing 11-7.*** The command to build a Maven project

```
mvn package
```

If everything has been configured correctly, you should see a console printout similar to the following:

```
[INFO] -------------------------------------------------------------
[INFO] BUILD SUCCESS
[INFO] -------------------------------------------------------------
[INFO] Total time:  1.644 s
[INFO] Finished at: 2020-11-01T05:17:25-06:00
[INFO] -------------------------------------------------------------
```

# Show Me the Code

You can find a complete, fully compilable sample application in the GitHub repository dedicated to this book. Simply navigate to `https://github.com/apress/r2dbc-revealed` to either `git clone` or directly download the contents of the repository. From there you can find a sample application dedicated to this chapter in the ch11 folder.

# Looking Ahead

Now that you have a fundamental understanding of what Apache Maven is and a high-level view of its infrastructure and how dependencies are managed using it, you've gained a basic understanding of how an R2DBC driver can be added to an application.

In the next few chapters, we'll be building on the sample application you've created to showcase, in Java, how you can take advantage of R2DBC capabilities through integrations directly with the MariaDB R2DBC driver. As mentioned in the previous section, the sample application for this chapter and all of the remaining chapters can be found in the GitHub repository dedicated to this book.

Also, as I mentioned earlier in this chapter, one of the goals of the R2DBC specification was to provide a path for creating more humane APIs through the use of R2DBC client libraries. So while the next several chapters will be focused on integrating direction with an R2DBC driver, Chapter 16 will take a closer look at what it's like to use the Spring Data R2DBC client library to develop fully reactive applications. Basically, if you love code, you're going to love the next several chapters!

# Summary

In this chapter, you learned about the different R2DBC driver and client solutions that are currently available. You also gained an understanding of how those solutions have been made available either directly through their open source code or as a Maven-based package.

Finally, you walked through the process of creating a Java project that includes both an R2DBC driver and client which will be used in subsequent chapters to examine the capabilities of reactive interactions with the relational database, MariaDB.

# CHAPTER 12

# Managing Connections

In the previous chapter, you were introduced to the process of creating a new Java project and, utilizing the capabilities of Apache Maven, adding the MariaDB R2DBC driver as a dependency to the project. Now that you've successfully created an application capable of taking advantage of an R2DBC implementation, it's time to dive into the capabilities of the specification.

In this chapter, we're going to expand on that project to examine the Connection object implementations available in the driver. Before continuing, if you haven't done so yet, I highly recommend reading Chapter 4, which dives into much greater detail on the R2DBC specification connection hierarchy and workflow.

## Configuration

For the purposes of this chapter, I'm going to be highlighting what I would consider *conventional* connection parameters for examples of how to establish a connection to MariaDB. More specifically, I'll be providing examples that target a *local* database instance.

---

**Note**  To run a program locally means to run it on the machine you are sitting at (or to run it on the same machine it is running on itself), as opposed to causing it to run on some remote machine.

---

Beyond this sample, if you'd like more information on the configuration options available for MariaDB, or any other DBMS, I highly suggest checking out the official MariaDB documentation.

© Robert Hedgpeth 2021
R. Hedgpeth, *R2DBC Revealed*, https://doi.org/10.1007/978-1-4842-6989-3_12

# Database Connectivity

In the last chapter, we walked through the process of getting a database instance up and running on your machine. This was done so that you have access to a MariaDB database instance that you can use to test the capabilities of the MariaDB R2DBC driver. I specifically provided guidance on setting up a local database instance as it requires minimal configuration information in order to establish a connection.

For instance, in Table 12-1, I've indicated the information necessary to connect to a local instance of MariaDB.

***Table 12-1.*** *Sample connection parameters*

| Property | Value | Description |
| --- | --- | --- |
| Hostname | 127.0.0.1 | The IP address, or domain, of your MariaDB Server. The default IP address for a local database instance is 127.0.0.1. |
| Port | 3306 | Port numbers are used as a way to identify how specific processes are to be forwarded. The default port number for MariaDB is 3306. |
| Username | app_user | The username needed to connect to a MariaDB database instance. |
| Password | Password123! | The password needed to connect to a MariaDB database instance. |

**Note**    In Chapter 11, I provided SQL statements for creating a new user, app_user, with the password Password123! for a MariaDB database instance. While it's certainly possible to use any credentials you want, for the sake of simplicity and consistency, I will be using app_user for all connection code settings in this book.

# Driver Implementation and Extensibility

As you can see in Table 12-1, the information is minimal. This helps you on two fronts. One, it provides you with the simplest approach to connecting to a MariaDB database. And, two, the requirement of a host, port number, username, and password is something that is common among all other relational databases and, thus, is an example that can be applied to other database vendors and their corresponding R2DBC driver implementations.

# Running Reactive Code

Before continuing, it's important to note that many of the examples going forward in this book will be using *non-blocking* method execution, such as the subscribe method.

Because we will be using a simple console application, which utilizes a single class and main method, it's possible, due to the nature of asynchronous event-driven communication, that the application may complete execution before publishers send information to their subscribers.

As a possible workaround, and an approach I'll be utilizing throughout the next several chapters, code can be added to keep the application running by blocking the current thread.

First, modify the main method to allow for throwing an InterruptedException. Doing so will allow you to add code to join the current thread, which will prevent the main method from exiting (Listing 12-1).

*Listing 12-1.* Keep the current thread threading to allow time for publishers and subscribers to complete processing

```
public static void main(String[] arg     s) throws InterruptedException {
    // This is where we'll be executing R2DBC sample code

    Thread.currentThread().join();
}
```

---

**Caution**   The code block from Listing 12-1 is merely a workaround for demonstration purposes. It is unlikely that you'll want to use such code within more practical, or "real-world," solutions.

---

# Establishing Connections

In Chapter 4, you learned that the creation of R2DBC Connection object implementations is managed through ConnectionFactory object implementations of a driver.

Before proceeding, it's important to note that the MariaDB R2DBC driver implements the full hierarchy of connection interfaces and provides a simple naming convention for each of the objects by preceding the names of each object with "Mariadb." Thus, the driver implements the `Connection` and `ConnectionFactory` interfaces as `MariadbConnection` and `MariadbConnectionFactory`, respectively.

---

**Note**   This type of naming convention is common for other R2DBC driver implementations.

---

# Obtaining MariadbConnectionFactory

Above all else, the `MariadbConnectionFactory` object is used to manage `MariadbConnection` objects. Of course, in order to be able to manage `MariadbConnection` objects, they need to exist, and before that you'll need to get your hands on a `ConnectionFactory` implementation. The MariaDB driver provides three approaches for obtaining `MariadbConnectionFactory`.

## Creating a New Connection Factory

One approach is to use the `MariadbConnectionConfiguration` object, which allows you to provide a variety of information, such as the host address, port number, username, and password, to identify a target MariaDB server instance. The `MariadbConnectionFactory` object can then be constructed using a `MariadbConnectionConfiguration` instance (Listing 12-2).

***Listing 12-2.*** Creating a new MariadbConnectionFactory object using MariadbConnectionConfiguration

```
MariadbConnectionConfiguration connectionConfiguration =
MariadbConnectionConfiguration.builder()
                    .host("127.0.0.1")
                    .port(3306)
                    .username("app_user")
                    .password("Password123!")
                    .build();

MariadbConnectionFactory connectionFactory = new MariadbConnectionFactory(
connectionConfiguration);
```

# MariadbConnectionConfiguration

The MariadbConnectionConfiguration class is specific to the MariaDB driver in that it doesn't derive from or implement an entity that exists within the R2DBC SPI.

However, the [DriverName]ConnectionConfiguration object is common among every driver implementation to date, but not only because of the naming convention. Connection configuration objects function to manage both standard and vendor-specific connectivity options.

Once a ConnectionConfiguration object is created, there are a variety of get methods you can use to read its current configuration settings (Listing 12-3).

***Listing 12-3.*** Example MariadbConnectionConfiguration getter method usages

```
// Where connectionConfiguration is an existing
MariadbConnectionConfiguration object
String host = connectionConfiguration.getHost();
int post = connectionConfiguration.getPort();
String username = connectionConfiguration.getUsername();
int prepareCacheSize = connectionConfiguration.getPrepareCacheSize();
```

Connection configuration objects also provide a sort of bridge, through ConnectionFactoryProvider implementations, to assist in the ConnectionFactory implementation discovery process using the ConnectionFactoryOptions class.

# ConnectionFactory Discovery

Harkening again back to Chapter 4, remember that ConnectionFactories, a class within the R2DBC SPI, provides two ways, both using the get method, to retrieve a driver ConnectionFactory implementation.

The first approach is to use a ConnectionFactoryOptions object to specify the appropriate connection settings for the target database instance (Listing 12-4).

***Listing 12-4.*** Retrieving an existing MariadbConnectionFactory object using a ConnectionFactoryOptions object

```
ConnectionFactoryOptions connectionFactoryOptions =
ConnectionFactoryOptions.builder()
                    .option(ConnectionFactoryOptions.DRIVER, "mariadb")
                    .option(ConnectionFactoryOptions.PROTOCOL, "pipes")
                    .option(ConnectionFactoryOptions.HOST, "127.0.0.1")
                    .option(ConnectionFactoryOptions.PORT, 3306)
                    .option(ConnectionFactoryOptions.USER, "app_user")
                    .option(ConnectionFactoryOptions.PASSWORD,
                    "Password123!").build();
MariadbConnectionFactory connectionFactory = (MariadbConnectionFactory)
ConnectionFactories.get(connectionFactoryOptions);
```

---

**Note**   Remember that in Chapter 11 I provided you with the SQL commands for adding a new user, app_user, to a MariaDB database instance.

---

Second, you also have the option of passing an R2DBC URL, which you learned about in Chapter 4, into ConnectionFactories' get method (Listing 12-5).

***Listing 12-5.*** Retrieving an existing MariadbConnectionFactory object using an R2DBC connection URL

```
MariadbConnectionFactory connectionFactory = (MariadbConnectionFactory)
ConnectionFactories.get("r2dbc:mariadb:pipes://app_user:Password123!
@127.0.0.1:3306");
```

Ultimately, the R2DBC URL is parsed to create a ConnectionFactoryOptions object that is then used by the ConnectionFactories class to obtain a ConnectionFactory just as it did in Listing 12-4.

# Creating a Connection

Once you've created a MariadbConnectionFactory object, you can then use the create method to obtain a MariadbConnection object (Listing 12-6).

*Listing 12-6.* Creating a new database connection

```
Mono<MariadbConnection> monoConnection = connectionFactory.create();

monoConnection.subscribe(connection -> {
    // Do something with connection
});
```

---

**Note**   A Mono is a Reactive Streams Publisher object implementation, provided by the Project Reactor library, with the specific intention of streaming *0–1* elements.

---

Notice that the ConnectionFactory interface's create method returns a Mono<MariadbConnection>, which is a Project Reactor implementation of the Reactive Streams API's Publisher<T> and the R2DBC specification's Publisher<Connection>.

And remember that due to the nature of event-based development, there's no telling *when* the MariadbConnection object will be published. Because of that, it may be useful, in certain situations, to wait for the publisher to send a Connection object before proceeding.

In such a scenario, you can use the block method to wait for a MariadbConnection object before proceeding (Listing 12-7).

*Listing 12-7.* Creating and waiting on a new database connection

```
MariadbConnection connection = connectionFactory.create().block();
```

# Validating and Closing Connections

After obtaining a MariadbConnection object, you can use the validate method to, yep, you guessed it, check whether the connection is still valid.

The validate method returns Publisher<Boolean>, which can be used by the Project Reactor library, using Mono.from, to create a Mono<Boolean> publisher. Then, as indicated in Listing 12-8, upon subscribing to monoValidated, the Boolean value, within the validated variable, can be used.

***Listing 12-8.*** Validating a connection

```
Publisher<Boolean> validatePublisher = connection.validate(ValidationDepth.
LOCAL);
            Mono<Boolean> monoValidated = Mono.from(validatePublisher);
            monoValidated.subscribe(validated -> {
                if (validated) {
                    System.out.println("Connection is valid");
                }
                else {
                    System.out.println("Connection is not valid");
                }
            });
```

**Note**   This example shows the usage of ValidationDepth.LOCAL, because of the local connection. For more information on ValidationDepth options, be sure to check out Chapter 4.

Likewise, the close method can be used to release the connection and its associated resources. In Listing 12-9, you can see how it's possible to subscribe to the close method.

***Listing 12-9.*** Closing a connection

```
Publisher<Void> closePublisher = connection.close();
Mono<Void> monoClose = Mono.from(closePublisher);
monoClose.subscribe();
```

# Putting It All Together

In Listing 12-10, I've accumulated all of the code snippets mentioned in this chapter into a single, runnable sample. The purpose of this sample is to demonstrate how to first establish a connection to the MariaDB database instance and then validate it. Then the connection will be closed and once more checked for validity.

*Listing 12-10.* The complete connection sample

```java
package com.example;

import org.mariadb.r2dbc.MariadbConnectionConfiguration;
import org.mariadb.r2dbc.MariadbConnectionFactory;
import org.mariadb.r2dbc.api.MariadbConnection;
import org.reactivestreams.Publisher;

import io.r2dbc.spi.ConnectionFactories;
import io.r2dbc.spi.ConnectionFactoryOptions;
import io.r2dbc.spi.ValidationDepth;
import reactor.core.publisher.Mono;

public class App
{
    public static void main( String[] args )
    {
        // Initialize Connection
        MariadbConnection connection = obtainConnection();

        // Validate Connection
        validateConnection(connection);

        // Close Connection
        closeConnection(connection);

        // Validate Connection
        validateConnection(connection);
    }

    public static MariadbConnection obtainConnection() {
        try {
            MariadbConnectionFactory connectionFactory;

            // Create a new Connection Factory using
            MariadbConnectionConfiguration
            connectionFactory = createConnectionFactory();
```

```
            // Discover Connection Factory using ConnectionFactoryOptions
            //connectionFactory = discoverConnectionFactoryWithConfiguration();

            // Discover Connection Factory using Url
            //connectionFactory = discoverConnectionFactoryWithUrl();

            // Create a MariadbConnection
            return connectionFactory.create().block();
        }
    catch (java.lang.IllegalArgumentException e) {
        printException("Issue encountered while attempting to obtain a
        connection", e);
        throw e;
        }
    }

    public static MariadbConnectionFactory createConnectionFactory() {
        try{
            // Configure the Connection
            MariadbConnectionConfiguration connectionConfiguration =
            MariadbConnectionConfiguration.builder()
                            .host("127.0.0.1")
                            .port(3306)
                            .username("app_user")
                            .password("Password123!")
                            .build();

            // Instantiate a Connection Factory
            MariadbConnectionFactory connectionFactory = new Mariadb
            ConnectionFactory(connectionConfiguration);

            print("Created new MariadbConnectionFactory");

            return connectionFactory;
        }
```

```
        catch(Exception e) {
            printException("Unable to create a new
            MariadbConnectionFactory", e);
            throw e;
        }
    }

    public static MariadbConnectionFactory
    discoverConnectionFactoryWithConfiguration() {
        try{
            ConnectionFactoryOptions connectionFactoryOptions =
            ConnectionFactoryOptions.builder()
                .option(ConnectionFactoryOptions.DRIVER, "mariadb")
                .option(ConnectionFactoryOptions.PROTOCOL, "pipes")
                .option(ConnectionFactoryOptions.HOST, "127.0.0.1")
                .option(ConnectionFactoryOptions.PORT, 3306)
                .option(ConnectionFactoryOptions.USER, "app_user")
                .option(ConnectionFactoryOptions.PASSWORD, "Password123!")
                .option(ConnectionFactoryOptions.DATABASE, "todo")
                .build();

            MariadbConnectionFactory connectionFactory =
            (MariadbConnectionFactory)ConnectionFactories.
            get(connectionFactoryOptions);

            return connectionFactory;
        }
        catch(Exception e) {
            printException("Unable to discover MariadbConnectionFactory
            using ConnectionFactoryOptions", e);
            throw e;
        }
    }
```

```
public static MariadbConnectionFactory
discoverConnectionFactoryWithUrl() {
    try {
        MariadbConnectionFactory connectionFactory =
        (MariadbConnectionFactory)ConnectionFactories.
        get("r2dbc:mariadb:pipes://app_user:Password123!
        @127.0.0.1:3306/todo");
        return connectionFactory;
    }
    catch (Exception e) {
        printException("Unable to discover MariadbConnectionFactory
        using Url", e);
        throw e;
    }
}

public static void validateConnection(MariadbConnection connection) {
    try {
        Publisher<Boolean> validatePublisher = connection.
        validate(ValidationDepth.LOCAL);
        Mono<Boolean> monoValidated = Mono.from(validatePublisher);
        monoValidated.subscribe(validated -> {
            if (validated) {
                print("Connection is valid");
            }
            else {
                print("Connection is not valid");
            }
        });
    }
    catch (Exception e) {
        printException("Issue encountered while attempting to verify a
        connection", e);
    }
}
```

```
public static void closeConnection(MariadbConnection connection) {
    try {
        Publisher<Void> closePublisher = connection.close();
        Mono<Void> monoClose = Mono.from(closePublisher);
        monoClose.subscribe();
    }
    catch (java.lang.IllegalArgumentException e) {
        printException("Issue encountered while attempting to verify a
        connection", e);
    }
}

public static void printException(String description, Exception e) {
    print(description);
    e.printStackTrace();
}

public static void print(String val) {
    System.out.println(val);
}
}
```

Successfully running the sample code in Listing 12-10 should yield a result similar to that indicated in Listing 12-11.

***Listing 12-11.*** The resulting output from executing the code in Listing 12-10

```
Connection is valid
Connection is not valid
```

The code in Listing 12-10, while very simple, provides foundational connection functionality that I'll continue to expand on in upcoming chapters.

# Metadata

Lastly, it's possible to inspect information, or metadata, about the ConnectionFactory and Connection object implementations (Listing 12-12, Listing 12-13).

The MariadbConnectionFactoryMetadata object exposes a single method, getName, that returns the name of the product that R2DBC is connected to.

*Listing 12-12.* Using MariadbConnectionFactoryMetadata

```
ConnectionFactoryMetadata metadata = connectionFactory.getMetadata();
String name = metadata.getName();
```

You also have the ability, as indicated in Listing 12-13, to retrieve metadata about an established connection using the MariadbConnection object. The MariadbConnectionMetadata object implements the ConnectionMetadata interface, as well as its required methods. MariadbConnectionMetadata also exposes several additional methods specific to the MariaDB driver implementation of R2DBC.

*Listing 12-13.* Using MariadbConnectionMetadata

```
MariadbConnectionMetadata metadata = connection.getMetadata();

// Methods required by the ConnectionMetadata interface
String productName = metadata.getDatabaseProductName();
String databaseVersion = metadata.getDatabaseVersion();

// Extension methods added to MariadbConnectionMetadata
boolean isMariaDBServer = metadata.isMariaDBServer();
int majorVersion = metadata.getMajorVersion();
int minorVersion = metadata.getMinorVersion();
int patchVersion = metadata.getPatchVersion();
```

# Show Me the Code

You can find a complete, fully compilable sample application in the GitHub repository dedicated to this book. If you haven't done so already, simply navigate to https:// github.com/apress/r2dbc-revealed to either git clone or directly download the contents of the repository. From there you can find a sample application dedicated to this chapter in the *ch12* folder.

# Summary

There's no doubt that the ability to connect to a data source is one of the, if not the most, important capabilities of a database driver. This chapter is crucial for taking the theoretical information you learned about in Chapter 4 and seeing it in action through the use of a driver implementation.

In this chapter, you gained an understanding of how to use the MariaDB R2DBC driver to create and manage database connections. The foundation provided in this chapter will be incredibly useful for upcoming chapters where we'll dive into concepts like statement execution, transaction management, connection pooling, and many more.

# CHAPTER 13

# Managing Data

So far, you've gained knowledge on the fundamentals of reactive programming, Reactive Streams, and R2DBC. And in the past two chapters, you've even had a first-hand look at how the R2DBC specification can come to life within a driver implementation. We've even created a simple application that uses the MariaDB R2DBC driver and connects to a database instance. This is where the real fun begins.

In this chapter, we're going to be expanding on the knowledge you've gained in the past two chapters to dive into executing SQL statements using the MariaDB R2DBC driver. Reads, writes, parameters, no parameters, yep, we're going to cover it.

Put simply, if you like code, you're going to love this chapter!

## MariadbStatement

Continuing with the convention of preceding the class names of R2DBC interfaces with *Mariadb*, the `MariadbStatement` object provides the ability to execute SQL statements on MariaDB databases.

## Statement Hierarchy

Figure 13-1 should look familiar. In Chapter 6, you learned that the R2DBC `Connection` interface exposes a method for obtaining a `Statement` object called `createStatement`. Thus, using the `MariadbConnection` object discussed in detail in the previous chapter, you can obtain a `MariadbStatement` object, which can then be used to execute SQL statements and access data through the `MariadbResult` object when applicable.

© Robert Hedgpeth 2021
R. Hedgpeth, *R2DBC Revealed*, https://doi.org/10.1007/978-1-4842-6989-3_13

*Figure 13-1.* *The MariaDB class flow for executing SQL statements*

## Dependency Disclaimer

In the last chapter, I pointed out that the MariaDB R2DBC driver contains a dependency on Project Reactor, a popular Reactive Streams implementation. Naturally, because of this, this chapter will provide many examples that use Project Reactor Reactive Streams class implementations.

However, please keep in mind, as I've stressed many times within this book, Reactive Streams is a specification so it's important to use the following examples as a guiding light, not just as a single source of truth for Reactive Streams implementations. There are a variety of options out there, many of which will function very similarly to the examples we'll be covering in this chapter.

# The Basics

There are a variety of ways that SQL can be executed and managed using the MariaDB R2DBC driver, which I hope to cover in this chapter. The intention of this section is to provide the foundation that we can build upon in subsequent sections as we navigate through the data management capabilities of an R2DBC driver.

## Creating Statements

It all starts by creating a Statement, or, in our case, the Statement implementation object provided by the MariaDB R2DBC driver: MariadbStatement.

Using a MariadbConnection object, you can obtain a new MariadbStatement object with the createStatement method, which takes a String value for the SQL statement you'd like to run (Listing 13-1).

*Listing 13-1.* Creating a new MariadbStatement using a MariadbConnection object

```
MariadbStatement createDatabaseStatement = connection.
createStatement("CREATE DATABASE todo");
```

## Obtaining a Publisher

Regardless of the implementation, the purpose of a Statement object's execute method is to provide a Reactive Streams Publisher<T> implementation, more specifically Publisher<Result> in this case.

So, by default, the MariadbStatement object's execute method provides a Flux<MariadbResult> (Listing 13-2).

*Listing 13-2.* Using the execute method on a Statement object to create a publisher

```
Flux<MariadbResult> publisher = createDatabaseStatement.execute();
```

---

**Note**   The Flux object is a Project Reactor implementation of the Reactive Streams Publisher interface. It functions to emit 0–N elements.

---

## Subscribing to Execution

The publisher object must be subscribed in order to initiate execution of the MariadbStatement object and the SQL statement contained therein.

*Listing 13-3.* Subscribing to a publisher

```
publisher.subscribe();
```

Putting everything together and rounding off this sample, the following example (Listing 13-4) illustrates how we add a new MariaDB table to our newly created database from Listings 13-2 and 13-3.

***Listing 13-4.*** Creating a table using R2DBC statement execution

```
MariadbStatement createTableStatement = connection.createStatement(
"CREATE TABLE todo.tasks (" +
                "id INT(11) unsigned NOT NULL AUTO_INCREMENT, " +
                "description VARCHAR(500) NOT NULL, " +
                "completed BOOLEAN NOT NULL DEFAULT 0, " +
                "PRIMARY KEY (id))"
            );
createTableStatement.execute().subscribe();
```

---

**Note**   This section used the creation of the *todo* database and *tasks* table to provide a simple example of how to execute SQL using an R2DBC driver. In the sections to follow, we'll be using SQL statements that utilize *todo.tasks*.

---

# Retrieving Results

Having gained a fundamental understanding of what it takes to create and execute SQL statements using R2DBC, it's time to crank things up a notch! Now, it's certainly possible that we could create applications that only involve running SQL statements that we don't expect to receive data back from, but that's not a very common scenario nor a very interesting one. It's much more likely that any applications we write will want to both write *and* read from an underlying database.

## Row Update Count

Starting simply, a handy mechanism that R2DBC provides is to retrieve the number of rows that have been affected by Data Manipulation Language (DML) statements.

---

**Note**   INSERT, UPDATE, and DELETE statements are all known as DML statements.

---

For DML statements, a subscriber can expect to receive a single `MariadbResult` object, which provides the `getRowsUpdated` method. Calling the `getRowsUpdated` method enables you to obtain a `Publisher<Integer>` object that, once subscribed, let's you acquire the number of rows affected by the executed SQL statement (Listing 13-5).

***Listing 13-5.*** Subscribing to a Statement object's getRowsUpdated method

```
MariadbStatement insertStatement = connection.createStatement("INSERT INTO
todo.tasks (description,completed) VALUES ('New Task 1',0)");

// Retrieve and print the number of rows affected
insertStatement.execute().subscribe(result -> result.getRowsUpdated().
subscribe(count -> System.out.println (count.toString())));
```

---

**Caution**   After emitting the update count, a `Result` object gets invalidated, and rows from the same `Result` object can no longer be consumed.

---

# Mapping Results

In the last sample, we used a `MariadbResult` object to get the number of rows affected by a SQL statement, but, as we learned in Chapter 7, that's really only the tip of the iceberg of what a `Result` object implementation contains.

The MariaDB R2DBC driver's `Result` object implementation, `MariadbResult`, provides data values and metadata (Figure 13-2).

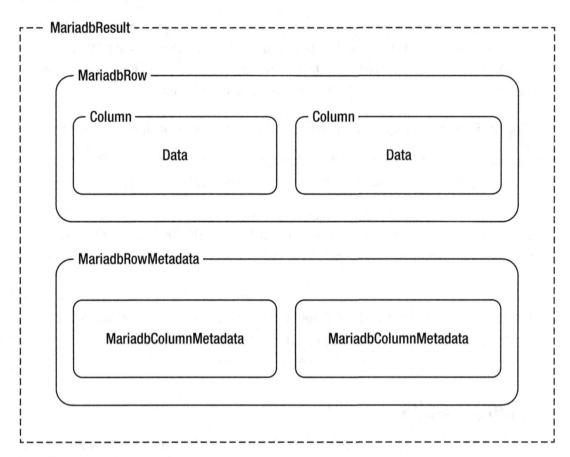

**Figure 13-2.**  *The anatomy of MariadbResult*

## Working with Row Objects

Recall that, in Chapter 7, you learned that the Result interface provides a map method for retrieving values from Row objects. Now that we're able to see this first-hand, it's worth elaborating a bit.

The process for Row object retrieval is possible because the map method accepts a BiFunction, also referred to as mapping function, object that accepts Row and RowMetadata.

---

**Note**   A BiFunction represents a function that accepts two arguments and produces a result (e.g., Row and RowMetadata).

---

The mapping function is called upon during row emission with Row and RowMetadata objects. Then, within the BiFunction object's function block, you can access the row object to extract data, per a specified column through the use of an index or column/alias name.

***Listing 13-6.*** Extracting SQL SELECT statement results using the MariadbRow get method

```
MariadbStatement selectStatement = connection.createStatement("SELECT id,
description AS task, completed FROM todo.tasks");

selectStatement.execute()
            .flatMap(result -> result.map((row,metadata) -> {
                Integer id = row.get(0, Integer.class);
                String descriptionFromAlias = row.get("task", String.
                class);
                String isCompleted = (row.get(2, Boolean.class) ==
                true) ? "Yes" : "No";
                return String.format("ID: %s - Description: %s -
                Completed: %s",
                    id,
                    descriptionFromAlias,
                    isCompleted
                );
            }))
            .subscribe(result -> System.out.println(result));
```

**Caution**    A Row is only valid during the mapping function callback and is invalid outside of the mapping function callback. Thus, Row objects must be entirely consumed by the mapping function.

## Mapping Results

The map and flatMap methods both receive a mapping function, which is applied to each element of a Stream<T> and returns a Stream<R>. The key difference between the two functions is that the mapping function that's received by the flatMap method produces a stream of *new* values, whereas the mapping function received by the map method is used to produce a single value for each input element.

And because the mapping function for the flatMap method is used to return a new stream, we essentially are receiving a stream of streams. However, the flatMap method is also used to replace each generated stream by the contents of that stream. In other words, all the separate streams that are generated by the function get flattened into one single stream.

## Handling Metadata

You may have noticed that the BiFunction in Listing 13-6 also includes an object named metadata, which is a MariadbRowMetadata object. In Chapter 8, you learned that the RowMetadata object implementations provide information about the tabular results returned from an executed SQL statement. More specifically, RowMetadata can be used to determine properties of a row and also exposes ColumnMetadata implementations for each column contained within the Result object.

In Listing 13-7, reusing the sample code from Listing 13-6, we can instead focus on extracting information from the metadata object.

*Listing 13-7.* Accessing row and column metadata

```
selectStatement.execute()
                    .flatMap(result -> result.map((row,metadata) -> {
                      List<String> columnMetadata = new
                      ArrayList<String>();
                      Iterator<String> iterator = metadata.
                      getColumnNames().iterator();
```

```
            while (iterator.hasNext()) {
                String columnName = iterator.next();
                columnMetadata.add(String.format(
                "%s (type=%s)", columnName, metadata.
                getColumnMetadata(columnName).
                getJavaType().getName()));
            }
            return columnMetadata.toString();
        }))
        .subscribe(result -> System.out.println(
        "Row Columns = "  + result));
```

# Generated Values

Next, let's consider the process of creating a *new* record using the Statement workflow we've learned about throughout this chapter.

*Listing 13-8.*  Inserting data

```
MariadbStatement insertStatement = connection.createStatement("INSERT INTO
todo.tasks (description,completed) VALUES ('New Task 2',0)");
insertStatement.execute().subscribe();
```

OK, so we've created a new MariadbStatement and subscribed to the execution of the contained INSERT statement. Great, but what if we want to get the value of the id that was auto-generated, per our table's specifications? Something about having to use mapping functions to simply gain access to auto-generated values seems cumbersome, verbose, and, well, just unnecessary. Sure, there's a better option.

Yep, R2DBC to the rescue yet again! If you recall, in Chapter 6, you were introduced to the returnGeneratedValues, a method available through the Statement interface that can be used to obtain auto-generated values that are created as part of a SQL statement. The method simply receives a variable-argument parameter that's used to pinpoint the column name that an auto-generated value is to be stored in.

***Listing 13-9.*** Retrieving a generated value from an INSERT statement execution

```
MariadbStatement insertStatement = connection.createStatement("INSERT INTO
todo.tasks (description,completed) VALUES ('New Task 3',0)");

Flux<Object> publisher =  insertStatement.returnGeneratedValues("id").
execute().flatMap(result -> result.map((row,metadata) -> row.get("id")));

 publisher.subscribe(id -> System.out.println
(id.toString()));
```

# Multiple Statements

As developers, we know that it's often useful, for a variety of reasons including the possibility to improve performance, to be able to execute multiple SQL statements during a single operation. Luckily, because of R2DBC's flexibility, there are a couple of ways to effectively *batch* SQL statements.

## Using MariadbBatch

The R2DBC SPI provides an interface called Batch that defines methods for running groups of parameter-less SQL statements.

---

**Stay Tuned**    Later in this chapter, we'll take a look at *parameterized* SQL statements that can be batched.

---

Thus, the MariaDB implementation, MariadbBatch, can be created and used to run multiple SQL statements, which can be helpful to improve application performance.

Start by creating an instance of MariadbBatch by using the createBatch method, which is available on a Connection object. Then use the add method to input each SQL statement you'd like to execute as part of the batch and use the execute method just like you would with a Statement object (Listing 13-10).

***Listing 13-10.*** Using MariadbBatch to execute multiple SQL statements

```
MariadbBatch batch = connection.createBatch();
```

```
batch.add("INSERT INTO todo.tasks (description,completed) VALUES (
'New Task 4', 0)")
    .add("SELECT * FROM todo.tasks WHERE id = last_insert_id()")
    .execute()
    .flatMap(result -> result.map((row,metadata) -> {
                return row.get(0, Integer.class)  + " - " + row.get(
                1, String.class);
    }))
    .subscribe(result -> System.out.println(result));
```

## Using MariadbStatement

Due to the flexibility offered by the R2DBC specification, the MariaDB R2DBC driver also makes it possible to include multiple SQL statements within a single String value used to construct a Statement object.

First, there is a vendor-specific method called allowMultiQueries that needs to be included during the building process of the MariadbConnectionConfiguration object that's used to create the MariadbConnection used to execute SQL statements (Listing 13-11).

***Listing 13-11.*** Enabling the ability to run multiple SQL statements in a single Statement object execution using allowMultiQueries

```
MariadbConnectionConfiguration connectionConfiguration =
MariadbConnectionConfiguration.builder()
    .host("127.0.0.1")
    .port(3306)
    .username("app_user")
    .password("Password123!")
    .allowMultiQueries(true)
    .build();
```

Once you've enabled the ability to execute multiple SQL queries, you are able to add multiple queries, within a single String value, separated by a semicolon (Listing 13-12).

***Listing 13-12.*** Running multiple INSERT statements within a single Statement object execution

```
MariadbStatement multiStatement = connection.createStatement("INSERT INTO
todo.tasks (description,completed) VALUES ('New Task 5', 0); SELECT * FROM
todo.tasks WHERE id = last_insert_id();");

multiStatement.execute().flatMap(result -> result.map((row,metadata) -> {
                         return row.get(0, Integer.class)  + " - " +
                         row.get(1, String.class);
                       }))
                       .subscribe(result -> System.out.println(result));
```

# Parameterized Statements

In Chapter 6, you learned that the same *non-parameterized* SQL String values that are used to create a Statement object can also be *parameterized* by using vendor-specific bind markers. In fact, parameterized Statement objects are created by Connection objects in the same way as non-parameterized statements.

In fact, as I pointed out in Chapter 6, the bind markers used by vendors can differ, but the overall approach is the same. For MariaDB, you have two bind marker options:

1. By using a single question mark (?) as a parameter placeholder

2. By preceding a named parameter placeholder with a semicolon (:)

## Binding Parameters

Regardless of the bind marker used, you can supply an index number of the parameter to bind a value to (Listing 13-13).

***Listing 13-13.*** Binding by index

```
MariadbStatement selectStatement = connection.createStatement("SELECT *
FROM todo.tasks WHERE completed = ? AND id >= ?");
selectStatement.bind(0, true);
selectStatement.bind(1, 4);
```

```
selectStatement.execute()
            .flatMap(result -> result.map((row,metadata) -> {
                return row.get(0, Integer.class)  + " - " + row.get(
                1, String.class) + " - " + row.get(2, Boolean.class);
            }))
            .subscribe(result -> System.out.println(result));
```

You can also supply a specific placeholder parameter (Listing 13-14).

***Listing 13-14.*** Binding with a named placeholder

```
MariadbStatement selectStatement = connection.createStatement("SELECT *
FROM todo.tasks WHERE completed = :completed AND id >= :id");
selectStatement.bind("completed", true);
selectStatement.bind("id", 4);
selectStatement.execute()
            .flatMap(result -> result.map((row,metadata) -> {
                return row.get(0, Integer.class)  + " - " + row.get(1,
                String.class) + " - " + row.get(2, Boolean.class);
            }))
            .subscribe(result -> System.out.println(result));
```

# Batching Statements

In Chapter 6, you were also introduced to R2DBC's ability to support batched
parameterized Statement objects by taking advantage of the Statement object's add
method (Listing 13-15).

***Listing 13-15.*** Batching parameterized statements with MariadbStatement

```
MariadbStatement batchedInsertStatement = connection.createStatement("INSERT
INTO todo.tasks (description,completed) VALUES (?,?)");

batchedInsertStatement.bind(0, "New Task 6").bind(1, false).add();
batchedInsertStatement.bind(0, "New Task 7").bind(1, false).add();
batchedInsertStatement.bind(0, "New Task 8").bind(1, true);

batchedInsertStatement.execute().subscribe();
```

# Reactive Control

As you may recall from Chapter 2, the Reactive Streams API provides a structured process for managing event-driven development through asynchronous, non-blocking interactions. Basically, we learned that Reactive Streams adds some structure around the idea of wrangling data streams to help us create *fully* reactive applications.

By this point in the book, you've gained a solid understanding of the R2DBC specification and how it utilizes the Reactive Streams API to make reactive interactions with a relational database possible. Building on that, within this chapter and the last, you've also learned how an R2DBC driver implementation *actually* takes advantage of a Reactive Streams implementation to enable event-driven development.

While there are many Reactive Streams implementations and their approaches, class structure, and fine-grained functionality may vary, the overall premise remains the same. As you gain more experience and understanding as to how you'd like to utilize R2DBC, it's helpful to start with the basics.

## Blocking Execution

There are certain database interactions that will need to finish before you can complete subsequent operations. For instance, at the beginning of this chapter, I supplied a simple example (Listings 13-1 and 13-2) for creating a statement, executing a publisher, and subscribing to the result. But in order to be able to query on a database or table, it must first exist. For such a case, it may be useful to use one of the blocking functions within a *Flux* object (Listing 13-16).

*Listing 13-16.* Subscribing to a Flux and blocking indefinitely until the upstream signals its first value or completes

```
MariadbStatement createDatabaseStatement = connection.
createStatement("CREATE DATABASE todo");
createDatabaseStatement.execute().blockFirst();
```

---

**Note**    The blockFirst method subscribes to a Flux and blocks it indefinitely until the upstream signals its first value or completes.

---

156

On the other hand, if you have a batch of statements to execute, you also have the option to use the blockLast method.

***Listing 13-17.*** Subscribing to a Flux and blocking indefinitely until the upstream signals its last value or completes

```
MariadbStatement batchedInsertStatement = connection.createStatement("INSERT
INTO todo.tasks (description,completed) VALUES (?,?)");

batchedInsertStatement.bind(0, "New Task 9").bind(1, false).add()
                    .bind(0, "New Task 10").bind(1, false).add()
                    .bind(0, "New Task 11").bind(1, true);

MariadbResult result = batchedInsertStatement.execute().blockLast();
```

## Managing Back Pressure

Back in Chapter 1, you learned about the concept of *back pressure* and how it's crucial for controlling the flow of data in a reactive application. Then, Chapter 2 expanded on that understanding by learning about how the Reactive Streams API uses back pressure, through a formalized API structure, to enable non-blocking interactions (Figure 13-3).

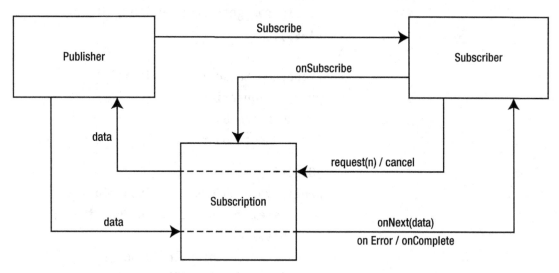

***Figure 13-3.***  *The Reactive Streams API workflow*

Though there are a variety of ways, architecturally speaking, that you could go about tapping into Reactive Streams capabilities to do things such as controlling back pressure, let's take a look at a simple example illustrating *one possible* approach.

In Listing 13-18, I've created a new MariadbStatement and used the flatMap method to return a task record's description value. Simple enough and should feel pretty familiar at this point. However, instead of simply using subscribe to obtain the values from the executed SQL statement, you'll notice that I have created a new Subscriber<String> object.

The following sample illustrates the relationship between a subscriber, subscription, and publisher. Examining the new subscriber, you can see that there are several overridden methods: onSubscribe, onNext, onError, and onComplete. These should look familiar as they coincide with the Reactive Streams API method functions elaborated on in Chapter 1 and from Figure 13-3.

***Listing 13-18.*** Controlling back pressure with a new Subscriber object

```
MariadbStatement selectStatement = connection.createStatement("SELECT *
FROM todo.tasks");
            selectStatement.execute()
                        .flatMap(result -> result.map((row,metadata) -> {
                            return row.get("description", String.
                            class);
                        }))
                        .subscribe(new Subscriber<String>() {
                            private Subscription s;
                            int onNextAmount;
                            int requestAmount = 2;

                            @Override
                            public void onSubscribe(Subscription s) {
                                System.out.println("onSubscribe");
                                this.s = s;
                                System.out.println("Request (" +
                                requestAmount + ")");
                                s.request(requestAmount);
                            }
```

```
@Override
public void onNext(String itemString) {
    onNextAmount++;
    System.out.println("onNext item
    received: " + itemString);
    if (onNextAmount % 2 == 0) {
        System.out.println("Request (" +
        requestAmount + ")");
        s.request(2);
    }
}

@Override
public void onError(Throwable t) {
    System.out.println("onError");
}

@Override
public void onComplete() {
    System.out.println("onComplete");
}
});
```

By creating a custom Subscriber object, of type String to account for our mapped result, you are able get a more in-depth look at the reactive interactions that have been facilitated between the MariaDB R2DBC driver and your application.

Notice that within Listing 13-18, I've included System.out.println usages to help illustrate the reactive flow. Executing the code should yield an output similar to Listing 13-19.

***Listing 13-19.*** Sample output for the custom subscriber in Listing 13-18

```
onSubscribe
Request (2)
onNext item received: Task 1
onNext item received: Task 2
```

```
Request (2)
onNext item received: Task 3
onNext item received: Task 4
Request (2)
onNext item received: Task 5
onComplete
```

## Show Me the Code

You can find a complete, fully compilable sample application in the GitHub repository dedicated to this book. If you haven't done so already, simply navigate to https://github.com/apress/r2dbc-revealed to either git clone or directly download the contents of the repository. From there you can find a sample application dedicated to this chapter in the *ch13* folder.

## Summary

Whew! We were able to cover quite a bit of ground in this chapter. We started by taking a look at the basics of utilizing the Statement object implementation, MariadbStatement, to facilitate reactive SQL statement execution. From there you expanded your knowledge by gaining an understanding of how SQL statement results are handled.

Parameters, no parameters, we pretty much covered it all! Finally, you even got a taste of what it's like to be able to control the event-driven, fully reactive flow of information using R2DBC and the concept of back pressure.

# CHAPTER 14

# Managing Transactions

In Chapter 5, you were introduced, or possibly reintroduced, to the basic concepts of transactions and their significance within relational database solutions. Most importantly, you gained an understanding of the transactional feature support that the R2DBC specification provides.

In this chapter, we'll be using the MariaDB R2DBC driver to get a first-hand look at what it takes to create, manage, and utilize transactions in a reactive solution.

## Database Transaction Support

Among the differences that exist between different relational database solutions is the number of transactional features they support. In Chapter 5, you learned the transactional capabilities that are available within the R2DBC specification.

Continuing with the trend we've set in the past few previous chapters; we're going to take a look at those capabilities in action using the MariaDB R2DBC driver. We're going to avoid diving into the intricacies of MariaDB-specific features, instead covering what is possible using R2DBC.

## Database Preparation

Going forward, we're going to be looking at Java code examples, using the MariaDB R2DBC driver, that rely on a SQL table, called *tasks*, that exists in a database, *todo*, that we added to a MariaDB instance in the last chapter.

To get us on the same page, you can execute the SQL in Listing 14-1 to reset the *todo. tasks* table.

© Robert Hedgpeth 2021
R. Hedgpeth, *R2DBC Revealed*, https://doi.org/10.1007/978-1-4842-6989-3_14

*Listing 14-1.* Truncating the existing records and adding new records to todo. tasks

```
TRUNCATE TABLE todo.tasks; INSERT INTO todo.tasks (description) VALUES
('Task A'), ('Task B'), ('Task C');
```

---

**Tip**    In SQL, the TRUNCATE  TABLE statement is a Data Definition Language (DDL) operation that marks the extents of a table for deallocation. Truncating the tasks table will remove all preexisting information as well restart the auto-generated value count for the *id* column.

---

Executing SQL in Listing 14-1 will ensure that our table contains three records, containing id column values of 1, 2, and 3, respectively.

*Listing 14-2.* The contents of todo.tasks after executing the SQL in Listing 14-1

```
+----+-------------+-----------+
| id | description | completed |
+----+-------------+-----------+
|  1 | Task A      |         0 |
|  2 | Task B      |         0 |
|  3 | Task C      |         0 |
+----+-------------+-----------+
```

# Transaction Basics

The R2DBC specification provides support for controlling transactional operations via code, as opposed to using SQL directly, through the Connection interface, which all drivers are required to implement.

Transactions can be started implicitly or explicitly. When a Connection object is in auto-commit mode, transactions are started *implicitly* when a SQL statement is executed through a Connection object.

# Auto-committing

In Chapter 5, you learned that the auto-commit mode of a Connection object can be retrieved using the isAutoCommit method and changed by invoking the setAutoCommit method (Listing 14-3).

***Listing 14-3.*** Disabling auto-commit for a Connection object

```
boolean isAutoCommit = connection.isAutoCommit();
if (isAutoCommit) {
      connection.setAutoCommit(false).block();
}
```

---

**Tip**   Auto-commit is *enabled* by default within the MariaDB R2DBC driver.

---

# Explicit Transactions

Once the auto-commit mode is disabled, transactions must be *explicitly* started. Using the MariaDB driver, this can be accomplished by invoking the beginTransaction method on a MariadbConnection object (Listing 14-4).

***Listing 14-4.*** Beginning a MariaDB transaction

```
connection.beginTransaction().subscribe();
```

---

**Tip**   Using the beginTransaction method on a MariadbConnection object will automatically disable *auto-commit* for the connection.

---

# Committing a Transaction

Once you've started down the path of explicitly handling a database transaction, no matter how many SQL statements you've created and executed, you will need to call the commitTransaction method to make the changes to the data permanent (Listing 14-5).

***Listing 14-5.*** Beginning and committing a MariaDB transaction

```
MariadbStatement insertStatement = connection.createStatement("INSERT INTO
tasks (description) VALUES ('Task D'));

insertStatement.execute()
              .then(connection.commitTransaction())
              .subscribe();
```

---

**Note**   In Listing 14-5, the then method, provided by *Project Reactor*, is used to set up chained, declarative interactions.

---

Executing the code in Listing 14-5 will result in a new task row being added to the *tasks* table. The INSERT statement's change becomes permanent when the transaction is committed. You can confirm the results by taking a look at the contents within the tasks table (Listing 14-6).

***Listing 14-6.*** Output that results after committing the transaction

```
SELECT * FROM todo.tasks;
+----+-------------+-----------+
| id | description | completed |
+----+-------------+-----------+
|  1 | Task A      |         0 |
|  2 | Task B      |         0 |
|  3 | Task C      |         0 |
|  4 | Task D      |         0 |
+----+-------------+-----------+
```

## Rolling Back a Transaction

However, if there is a scenario that requires you to reverse the SQL statement or, for some reason, the transaction fails, it can all be rolled back by executing and subscribing to the rollbackTransaction method (Listing 14-7).

***Listing 14-7.*** Rolling back a MariaDB transaction

```
connection.rollbackTransaction().subscribe();
```

Executing the code in Listing 14-7 will roll back the INSERT statement's change, preventing it from being committed. When this happens, the contents of the *tasks* table will look like Listing 14-8.

**Listing 14-8.** Output that results after rolling back the transaction

```
SELECT * FROM todo.tasks;
+----+-------------+-----------+
| id | description | completed |
+----+-------------+-----------+
|  1 | Task A      |         0 |
|  2 | Task B      |         0 |
|  3 | TASK C      |         0 |
+----+-------------+-----------+
```

# An Imperative Perspective

Think back to Chapter 1, where you learned about imperative and declarative programming. As a refresher, remember that *blocking* operations are common within the *imperative*, or step-by-step, programming paradigm and languages. By contrast, declarative approaches do not focus on *how* to accomplish a specific goal but rather the goal itself.

And, by now, you know that the intention of R2DBC, and reactive programming as a whole, is to provide a *declarative* solution. That being said, sometimes it's easier for our brains to understand more of an imperative flow.

In an effort to most clearly lay out a transactional workflow, I've taken advantage of the block and blockLast methods in Listing 14-9, something you'd likely not do in a truly reactive application but helps to illustrate what's happening a little more clearly.

**Listing 14-9.** Handling exceptions and transactions

```
try {
    connection.beginTransaction().block();

    MariadbStatement multiStatement = connection.createStatement(
    "DELETE FROM tasks; INSERT INTO tasks (description) VALUES ('Task D');
    SELECT * FROM tasks;");
```

```
multiStatement.execute().blockLast();

    connection.commitTransaction().subscribe();
}
catch(Exception e) {
    connection.rollbackTransaction().subscribe();
    // More exception handling code
}
```

Listing 14-9 takes advantage of the MariaDB R2DBC driver's ability to execute multiple SQL statements within a single `MariadbStatement` object.

---

**Tip**    See Chapter 13 for more information on this.

---

***Listing 14-10.*** After successfully committing the transactions from Listing 14-9

```
SELECT * FROM todo.tasks;
+----+-------------+-----------+
| id | description | completed |
+----+-------------+-----------+
|  4 | Task D      |         0 |
+----+-------------+-----------+
```

***Listing 14-11.*** Encountering an exception and rolling back the transactions from Listing 14-9

```
SELECT * FROM todo.tasks;
+----+-------------+-----------+
| id | description | completed |
+----+-------------+-----------+
|  1 | Task A      |         0 |
|  2 | Task B      |         0 |
|  3 | Task C      |         0 |
+----+-------------+-----------+
```

# Managing Savepoints

In Chapter 5, you learned that savepoints can be useful when it is necessary to roll back part of a transaction. This is usually the case when there is a low possibility of error in part of the transaction and the prior validation of the operation's accuracy is too costly.

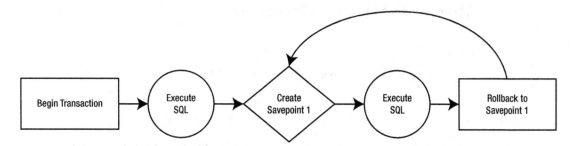

***Figure 14-1.*** *The basic workflow of a savepoint*

# Using Savepoints

Using the MariaDB driver, savepoints can be created using the `createSavepoint` method, available within a `MariadbConnection` object.

***Listing 14-12.*** Chaining subscribers to commit transactions

```
Boolean rollbackToSavepoint = true;

MariadbStatement insertStatement = connection.createStatement("INSERT INTO
tasks (description) VALUES ('TASK X');");

MariadbStatement deleteStatement = pconnection.createStatement("DELETE FROM
tasks WHERE id = 2;");

insertStatement.execute().then(connection.createSavepoint("savepoint_1").
then(deleteStatement.execute().then(rollBackOrCommit(connection,rollbackTo
Savepoint)))).subscribe();
```

In this scenario, the `rollbackOrCommit` method, used in Listing 14-12, contains conditional functionality that either rolls back a transaction to *savepoint_1* and then commits the transaction or commits the entire transaction.

***Listing 14-13.*** The rollbackOrCommit method

```
private Mono<Void> rollBackOrCommit(MariadbConnection connection, Boolean
rollback) {
        if (rollback) {
            return connection.rollbackTransactionToSavepoint("savepoint_1")
            .then(connection.commitTransaction());
        }
        else {
            return connection.commitTransaction();
        }
}
```

Listing 14-14 contains a more imperative approach to Listings 14-12 and 14-13.

***Listing 14-14.*** Blocked equivalent of Listings 14-12 and 14-13

```
Boolean rollbackToSavepoint = true;

MariadbStatement insertStatement = connection.createStatement("INSERT INTO
tasks (description) VALUES ('TASK D');");
insertStatement.execute().blockFirst();

connection.createSavepoint("savepoint_1").block();

MariadbStatement deleteStatement = connection.createStatement("DELETE FROM
tasks WHERE id = 2;");
deleteStatement.execute().blockFirst();

if (rollbackToSavepoint) {
    connection.rollbackTransactionToSavepoint("savepoint_1").block();
}

connection.commitTransaction();
```

Whether you use the declarative approach from Listings 14-12 and 14-13 or the imperative flow in Listing 14-14, the output will be the same, as indicated in Listings 14-15 and 14-16.

***Listing 14-15.*** Output that results after rolling back to savepoint_1

```
SELECT * FROM todo.tasks;
+----+-------------+-----------+
| id | description | completed |
+----+-------------+-----------+
|  1 | Task A      |         0 |
|  2 | Task B      |         0 |
|  3 | Task C      |         0 |
|  4 | Task D      |         0 |
+----+-------------+-----------+
```

***Listing 14-16.*** Output that results after committing the entire transaction

```
SELECT * FROM todo.tasks;
+----+-------------+-----------+
| id | description | completed |
+----+-------------+-----------+
|  1 | Task A      |         0 |
|  3 | Task C      |         0 |
|  4 | Task D      |         0 |
+----+-------------+-----------+
```

# Releasing Savepoints

Because savepoints allocate resources directly on the databases, database vendors may require that savepoints be released to dispose of resources. You learned in Chapter 5 that there are a variety of ways that savepoints will be deallocated, including through the use of the releaseSavepoint method (Listing 14-17).

***Listing 14-17.*** Release a savepoint

```
connection.releaseSavepoint("savepoint_1").subscribe();
```

# Handling Isolation Levels

Databases expose the ability to specify the level of isolation within transactions. The concept of transactional isolation defines the degree to which one transaction can be isolated from data or resource modification performed by other transactions, thereby impacting concurrent access while multiple transactions are active.

The `IsolationLevel` enumeration value can be retrieved by calling the `getTransactionIsolationLevel` method, available through a `MariadbConnection` object.

---

**Tip**   Head to Chapter 5 for more information on `IsolationLevel`.

---

***Listing 14-18.*** Getting the default MariaDB R2DBC driver IsolationLevel setting

```
IsolationLevel level = connection.getTransactionIsolationLevel();
```

---

**Note**   The default `IsolationLevel` value for the MariaDB storage engine, InnoDB, that has been used in these samples is REPEATABLE-READ.

---

To change the `IsolationLevel`, you can use the `setTransactionIsolationLevel` method, available through a `MariadbConnection` object.

***Listing 14-19.*** Changing the MariaDB R2DBC driver IsolationLevel setting

```
connection.setTransactionIsolationLevel(IsolationLevel.READ_UNCOMMITTED);
```

# Show Me the Code

You can find a complete, fully compilable sample application in the GitHub repository dedicated to this book. If you haven't already done so, simply navigate to https:// github.com/apress/r2dbc-revealed to either git clone or directly download the contents of the repository. From there you can find a sample application dedicated to this chapter in the *ch14* folder.

# Summary

The ability to use and control transactions is a key feature for building solutions that use relational databases. And that's because transactions are used to provide data integrity, isolation, correct application semantics, and a consistent view of data during concurrent database access.

In Chapter 5, you learned that R2DBC-compliant drivers are required to provide transaction support. In this chapter, you were able to see that in action. Using the MariaDB R2DBC driver, you learned how to create, commit, and roll back transactions. You also learned how to create and manage savepoints. And to finish things off, you saw how to handle isolation levels within a MariaDB database using R2DBC.

# CHAPTER 15

# Connection Pooling

Even with all of the advantages of reactive development and R2DBC we've dug through in this book, the fundamental process of opening a database is an expensive operation, especially if the target database is remote. The process of connecting to a database is expensive, in terms of resource utilization, because of the overhead of establishing a network connection and initializing the database connection. In turn, connection session initialization often requires time-consuming processing to perform user authentication and establish transactional contexts and other aspects of the session that are required for subsequent database usage.

So, in this chapter, we're going to take a look at the idea of connection pools. You'll gain an understanding of not only *what* connection pools are and *why* they can be necessary but also *how* they can be used within an R2DBC-based application to help improve application performance and efficiency.

## Connection Pool Fundamentals

Cutting to the chase, the concept of *pooling* connections helps by removing the need to constantly recreate and reestablish connections to the database. As seen in Figure 15-1, a connection pool functions as a cache of database Connection objects.

© Robert Hedgpeth 2021
R. Hedgpeth, *R2DBC Revealed*, https://doi.org/10.1007/978-1-4842-6989-3_15

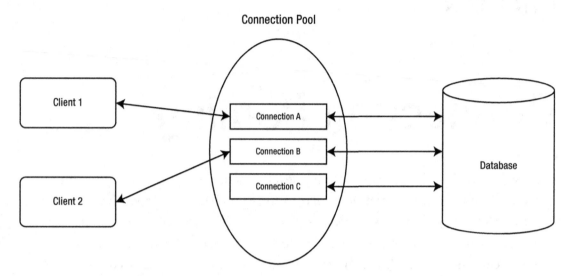

***Figure 15-1.*** *A simple connection pool workflow*

# Benefits of Connection Pooling

There are a variety of reasons you'd choose to implement a connection pool within an application, the most obvious being the ability to reuse existing connections. Reducing the number of connections that have to be created helps to provide several key advantages such as

- Reducing the number of times new Connection objects are created

- Promoting Connection object reuse

- Speeding up the process of obtaining a connection

- Reducing the amount of effort required to manage Connection objects

- Minimizing the number of stale connections

- Controlling the amount of resources spent on maintaining connections

Ultimately, the more database intensive an application is, the more it benefits from the use of connection pools.

# How to Get Started

We've learned that a key advantage of R2DBC is its extensibility, which is made possible through the specification's simplicity. In fact, it's so simple that you might have noticed that the idea of a connection pool hasn't been mentioned until this chapter. Out of the box, R2DBC does not provide support for connection pooling.

## Roll Your Own Connection Pool

R2DBC was built with extensibility in mind. With the specification mostly containing interfaces that require implementation, those implementations can be supplemented to include support for connection pooling. Basically, that means that R2DBC objects like `ConnectionFactory` and `Connection` can be created in such a way that, by default, includes support for connection pooling.

Of course, that's something that could be accomplished at the driver level, but, ideally, because of the generalized nature of the connection pooling concept, it might make more sense to support it as an independent, self-contained library.

Ultimately, it's out of the scope of this book to dive into the details on how connection pools can be created and maintained using a custom R2DBC implementation that has yet to be created. The real takeaway here is that it *can* be accomplished by creating an implementation from the R2DBC specification, located at `https://github.com/r2dbc/r2dbc-spi`, other libraries to help with the Reactive Streams implementation, and so on.

## Introducing R2DBC Pool

However, from a pragmatic perspective, developing support for connection pools from the ground up isn't trivial. For that reason, among others, it may be helpful to, instead of creating a custom solution, utilize an existing library for creating and managing connection pools. Luckily, such a library exists as a GitHub repository within the R2DBC account.

The *r2dbc-pool* project is a library that supports *reactive* connection pooling. Located at `https://github.com/r2dbc/r2dbc-pool`, the open source project uses the *reactor-pool* project, which provides functionality to support generic object pooling, as the foundation for fully non-blocking connection pooling.

---

**Note**    The *object pool pattern* is a software design pattern that uses a set, or a pool, of initialized objects kept ready to use rather than allocating and destroying them on command.

---

More specifically, and according to the reactor-pool documentation, the project aims to provide generic object pooling within reactive applications that

- Exposes a reactive API (`Publisher` input types, `Mono` return types)

- Is non-blocking (never blocking a user who makes an attempt to acquire a resource)

- Has lazy acquisition behavior

---

**Note**    Lazy loading, or acquisition, is a design pattern that focuses on deferring initialization of an object until the point at which it is needed.

---

The reactor-pool project is completely open source and can be found on GitHub at `https://github.com/reactor/reactor-pool`.

Going forward, we'll be using the r2dbc-pool project to examine how connection pools can be used to manage connections within an R2DBC-enabled application. Continuing with the trend that's been set in previous chapters, I'll be using the MariaDB R2DBC driver, in combination with r2dbc-pool, for all subsequent examples.

# R2DBC Pool

In this section, we're going to take a look at how the r2dbc-pool project can be used within an application to manage R2DBC connections.

## Adding a New Dependency

The r2dbc-pool artifact can be found on the Maven Central Repository, `https://search.maven.org/search?q=r2dbc-pool`, and can be added directly to an application's pom.xml file using the sample indicated in Listing 15-1.

***Listing 15-1.*** Adding the dependency for r2dbc-pool

```
<dependency>
  <groupId>io.r2dbc</groupId>
  <artifactId>r2dbc-pool</artifactId>
  <version>0.8.5.RELEASE</version>
</dependency>
```

> **Note**   You also have the option of using the latest version of r2dbc-pool by building directly from the source code. For more information, see the documentation at `https://github.com/r2dbc/r2dbc-pool`.

Before proceeding to the next section, it's important to reemphasize that the r2dbc-pool project does not provide any mechanisms for actually connecting to an underlying database. It needs to be used in combination with an existing driver to work. Going forward, I'll be providing examples that assume use of the MariaDB R2DBC driver that we've used in previous chapters.

## Connection Pool Configuration

You've learned that the `ConnectionFactoryOptions` object, which was first mentioned in Chapter 4 and then later in Chapter 12, exists to hold the configuration options used to, ultimately, create `ConnectionFactory` objects. The R2DBC Pool project extends the options available through `ConnectionFactoryOptions` to include discovery settings to support connection pools.

In Table 15-1, you can see the supported options, and correlating descriptions, for the connection pool settings exposed through R2DBC Pool.

*Table 15-1.* *Supported ConnectionFactory discovery options*

| Option | Description |
| --- | --- |
| driver | Must be *pool*. |
| protocol | Driver identifier. The value is propagated by the pool to the *driver* property. |
| acquireRetry | Number of retries if the first connection acquisition attempt fails. Defaults to 1. |
| initialSize | Initial number of Connection objects contained within a pool. Defaults to 10. |
| maxSize | Maximum number Connection objects contained within a pool. Defaults to 10. |
| maxLifeTime | Maximum lifetime of a connection within a pool. |
| maxIdleTime | Maximum idle time of a connection within a pool. |
| maxAcquireTime | Maximum allowed time to acquire a connection from a pool. |
| maxCreationConnectionTime | Maximum allowed time to create a new connection. |
| poolName | Name of the connection pool. |
| registerJMX | Whether to register the pool to JMX. |
| validationDepth | Validation depth used to validate an R2DBC connection. Defaults to LOCAL. |
| validationQuery | Query that will be executed just before a connection is received from the pool. Query execution is used to validate that a connection to the database is still alive. |

**Tip**   Java Management Extensions (JMX) is a Java technology that supplies tools for managing and monitoring applications, system objects, devices, and service-oriented networks. Those resources are represented by objects called MBeans. In the API, classes can be dynamically loaded and instantiated.

# Connection Factory Discovery

Ultimately, in order to be able to manage connections using a connection pool, you must have access to a ConnectionPool object. However, acquiring a ConnectionPool object starts by obtaining a ConnectionPool-compatible ConnectionFactory object. Creating a ConnectionPool-compatible ConnectionFactory object can be done in two ways.

First, you have the option of using an R2DBC URL. As indicated in Listing 15-2, a R2DBC URL that allows a ConnectionFactory object to be used by an R2DBC Pool ConnectionPool object requires the value *pool* for the driver and the value of *mariadb* for protocol.

***Listing 15-2.*** Using an R2DBC URL to discover a pool-capable ConnectionFactory

```
ConnectionFactory connectionFactory = ConnectionFactories.
get("r2dbc:pool:mariadb://app_user:Password123!@127.0.0.1:3306/
todo?initialSize=5");
Publisher<? extends Connection> connectionPublisher = connectionFactory.
create();
```

---

**Tip**    Other, optional, discovery options can be added after the question mark (?) in a R2DBC URL.

---

Alternatively, as indicated in Listing 15-3, you have the ability to programmatically create a new ConnectionFactory object using ConnectionFactoryOptions.

***Listing 15-3.*** Programmatically discovering a pool-capable ConnectionFactory

```
ConnectionFactoryOptions connectionFactoryOptions =
ConnectionFactoryOptions.builder()
.option(ConnectionFactoryOptions.DRIVER, "pool")
.option(ConnectionFactoryOptions.PROTOCOL, "mariadb")
.option(ConnectionFactoryOptions.HOST, "127.0.0.1")
.option(ConnectionFactoryOptions.PORT, 3306)
```

```
.option(ConnectionFactoryOptions.USER, "app_user")
.option(ConnectionFactoryOptions.PASSWORD, "Password123!")
.option(ConnectionFactoryOptions.DATABASE, "todo")
 .build();
```

## ConnectionPoolConfiguration

A ConnectionFactory object is then used to create a ConnectionPoolConfiguration object (Listing 15-4).

***Listing 15-4.*** Building a ConnectionPoolConfiguration object using ConnectionFactory

```
ConnectionPoolConfiguration configuration = ConnectionPoolConfiguration.
builder(connectionFactory)
            .maxIdleTime(Duration.ofMillis(1000))
            .maxSize(5)
            .build();
```

## Creating a ConnectionPool

The preceding sections described the workflow for creating a ConnectionPoolConfiguration object, which is necessary for creating a new ConnectionPool object (Listing 15-5).

***Listing 15-5.*** Creating a new connection pool

```
ConnectionPool connectionPool = new ConnectionPool(configuration);
```

The ConnectionPool object is simply a custom implementation of the R2DBC SPI ConnectionFactory interface (Listing 15-6), which is how it, as we'll see in the next section, makes it possible to obtain Connection objects.

***Listing 15-6.*** Class implementation of ConnectionPool

```
public class ConnectionPool implements ConnectionFactory, Disposable,
Closeable, Wrapped<ConnectionFactory> {
...
}
```

# Managing Connections

We've learned that the R2DBC Connection object is the foundation that reactive interactions are built on and that in order to obtain a Connection object we have to go through a ConnectionFactory object.

In the previous section, we also learned that the R2DBC Pool project's ConnectionPool object is an implementation of the ConnectionFactory object.

## Obtaining a Connection

To take advantage of the connection pool management provided by the R2DBC Pool project, you'll need to acquire Connection objects through a PooledConnection object.

The PooledConnection object is a custom implementation of the Connection interface (Listing 15-7).

***Listing 15-7.*** A high-level class implementation view of PooledConnection

```
final class PooledConnection implements Connection, Wrapped<Connection> {
...
}
```

Using the ConnectionPool object obtained in Listing 15-5, we can then access a Connection, more accurately a PooledConnection, object contained within the pool (Listing 15-8).

***Listing 15-8.*** Obtaining a PooledConnection object

```
PooledConnection pooledConnection = connectionPool.create().block();
```

Then, as expected, we can use the PooledConnection object to be able to communicate with the database to execute statements, manage transactions, and so on.

## Releasing a Connection

The purpose of a connection pool is to improve performance by using connections. For connections to be reused, they must be released back into the connection pool (Figure 15-2).

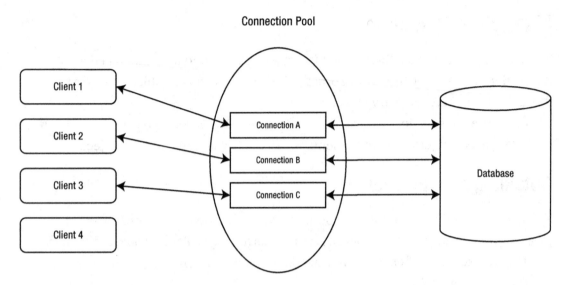

**Figure 15-2.** *All of the connections within a connection pool being used by clients*

Releasing a connection is the only way another client will be able to obtain and use a `Connection` object from a `ConnectionPool`, as seen in Figure 15-3.

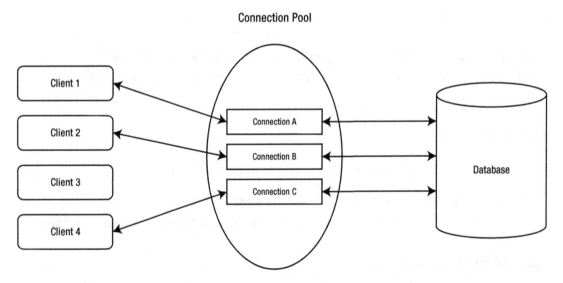

**Figure 15-3.** *After being released back into the connection pool, Connection C is available for Client 4 to use*

When a Connection object is no longer being used, it can be released back into the connection pool by calling the close method (Listing 15-9).

***Listing 15-9.*** Releasing a connection back into the connection pool

```
pooledConnection.close().subscribe();
```

## Cleaning Up

Along with the `ConnectionFactory` interface, the `ConnectionPool` object also implements the `Disposable` interface, which enables the ability to properly deallocate any and all resources it may be using by calling the `dispose` method (Listing 15-10).

***Listing 15-10.*** Disposing a connection pool

```
connectionPool.dispose();
```

Alternatively, you can use the `close` method, made available through the implementation of the `Closeable` interface (Listing 15-11).

***Listing 15-11.*** Closing a connection pool

```
connectionPool.close();
```

---

**Note**    Underneath the hood, the close method simply calls the dispose method.

---

# Show Me the Code

You can find a complete, fully compilable sample application in the GitHub repository dedicated to this book. If you haven't already done so, simply navigate to `https://github.com/apress/r2dbc-revealed` to either `git clone` or directly download the contents of the repository. From there you can find a sample application dedicated to this chapter in the *ch15* folder.

# Summary

Connection pools are essentially a cache of database connections maintained in the database's memory so that the connections can be reused when the database receives future requests for data. Ultimately connection pools are used to enhance the performance of executing commands on a database.

In this chapter, you gained a fundamental understanding of what connection pools are and how they can be extremely beneficial to use within applications, especially those with a large number of database-intensive operations. You learned about the R2DBC Pool project and gained first-hand knowledge of how to utilize it within an application.

# CHAPTER 16

# Practical Applications with Spring Data and R2DBC

So far, you've learned that R2DBC drivers provide a way to take advantage of the R2DBC API to utilize reactive code with relational databases. But you've likely noticed that there is quite a bit of work that is involved in creating a complete data access layer (DAL), which isn't something that is unique to R2DBC. In fact, one of the main benefits of R2DBC is that it doesn't aim to be a general-purpose data access API.

Instead, R2DBC focuses on reactive data access and common usage patterns that result from relational data interaction. Ultimately, R2DBC intends for common data access functionality to be the responsibility of R2DBC client libraries that were briefly mentioned in Chapter 11. In this chapter, we'll be examining a client library called Spring Data R2DBC, which is a part of the Spring application framework, to learn how an R2DBC client can help reduce the time and complexity of creating a fully reactive application.

## Introduction to Spring

Spring Framework is an application framework and Inversion of Control container for the Java platform. Spring Framework provides a comprehensive programming and configuration model for modern Java-based applications.

Throughout this chapter, I'll be utilizing Spring Framework, and libraries built on top of it, to illustrate how you can create a fully reactive web application that uses R2DBC through the Spring Data R2DBC client to interact with a relational database, more specifically MariaDB.

185

© Robert Hedgpeth 2021
R. Hedgpeth, *R2DBC Revealed*, https://doi.org/10.1007/978-1-4842-6989-3_16

# Spring Boot

Spring Boot is an open source Java framework that was developed by Pivotal, also a main contributor to R2DBC, and aims to simplify the task of developing and deploying Java enterprise web applications. It is a project built on top of Spring Framework.

> *Spring Boot makes it easy to create stand-alone, production-grade Spring based Applications that you can "just run".*
>
> —*Official Spring Boot Documentation*

To increase simplicity, the framework takes an opinionated stance on the Spring platform and third-party libraries for the sake of reducing developer configuration and code scaffolding.

In this chapter, we'll be examining a Spring Boot application. The application will expose an Application Programming Interface (API) through representational state transfer (REST) endpoints (Figure 16-1). Internally, the application will use the Spring Data R2DBC library in combination with the MariaDB R2DBC driver to connect to and communicate with the MariaDB database we set up in Chapter 11.

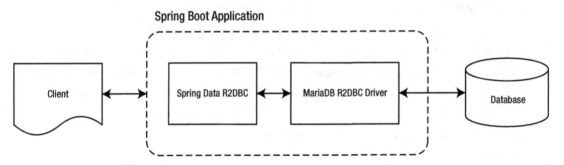

***Figure 16-1.*** *The Spring Boot application architecture*

For more information on Spring Boot, please check out the official documentation at https://spring.io/projects/spring-boot.

# Spring Data

Spring Data exists to unify and simplify the access to different kinds of persistence stores, both relational and non-relational. According to the official documentation, Spring Data's mission is to provide a familiar and consistent, Spring-based programming model for data access while still retaining the special traits of the underlying data store.

Because implementing the data access layer of an application can be cumbersome, often requiring a large amount of boilerplate code to be written, Spring Data provides repository abstraction to help reduce the effort needed to create data access and persistence layers.

A few of the key features I'll be utilizing in this chapter are

- Creating repository and custom object-mapping abstractions

- Dynamic query derivation from repository method names

- Customizing repository code

- Utilizing Spring integration via annotation

# Spring Data R2DBC

Similar to other Spring Data libraries, Spring Data R2DBC uses core Spring concepts to help with the development of solutions to integrate with a target data source. Like Spring Data JPA, which uses JDBC drivers, Spring Data R2DBC uses the R2DBC drivers to interact with relational databases and manage persistence using Spring Data repositories (Figure 16-2).

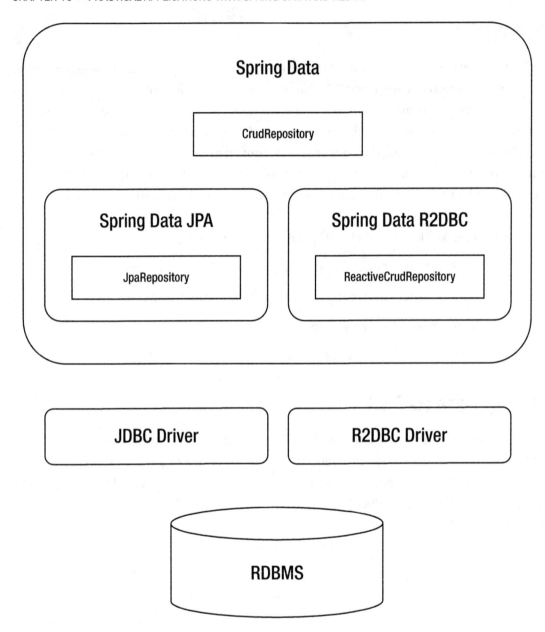

***Figure 16-2.*** *Spring Data R2DBC architecture*

## Project Reactor

By default, Spring Data R2DBC requires Project Reactor as a core dependency, but it is interoperable with other reactive libraries through the Reactive Streams specification.

Spring Data R2DBC repositories accept a Reactive Streams API `Publisher` as input and adapt it to a Project Reactor type internally to return either a `Mono` or a `Flux` output.

However, as we learned in previous chapters, any `Publisher` can be proved as input and apply operations on the output; the output will just need to be modified for use with another Reactive Streams API implementation library.

For the purposes of this chapter, I will stick to using the default, Project Reactor-based, outputs due to both Spring Data R2DBC and the MariaDB R2DBC connector sharing Project Reactor as a dependency.

# Getting Started

In Chapter 11, we walked through the process of creating a new Java application using the Apache Maven client. Hopefully this helped you gain an understanding of the fundamentals of creating a Java application that uses an R2DBC driver. In this chapter, I'll be focusing more on application code than on project infrastructure and, as such, will use a web application called Spring Initializr to generate a Java project containing various dependencies, including Spring Data R2DBC.

# Spring Initializr

Spring Initializr is a web application that can be used to generate a Spring Boot project structure for you. It doesn't generate any application code, but it will give you a basic project structure and either a Maven or a Gradle build specification to build your code with. All you need to do is write the application code.

The Spring Initializr project can be used in several ways, including

- A web-based interface

- Using the Spring Boot CLI

- Via Spring Tool Suite

---

**Note**   Spring Tool Suite (STS) is a set of tools for creating Spring applications. The toolset can be either installed as a plugin to an existing installation of Eclipse JEE or installed standalone.

---

However, for the sake of simplicity, I'll be walking through the web interface of Spring Initializr, hosted at `https://start.spring.io`. The web interface contains a single page that provides configurable options to generate a new Spring Boot application (Figure 16-3).

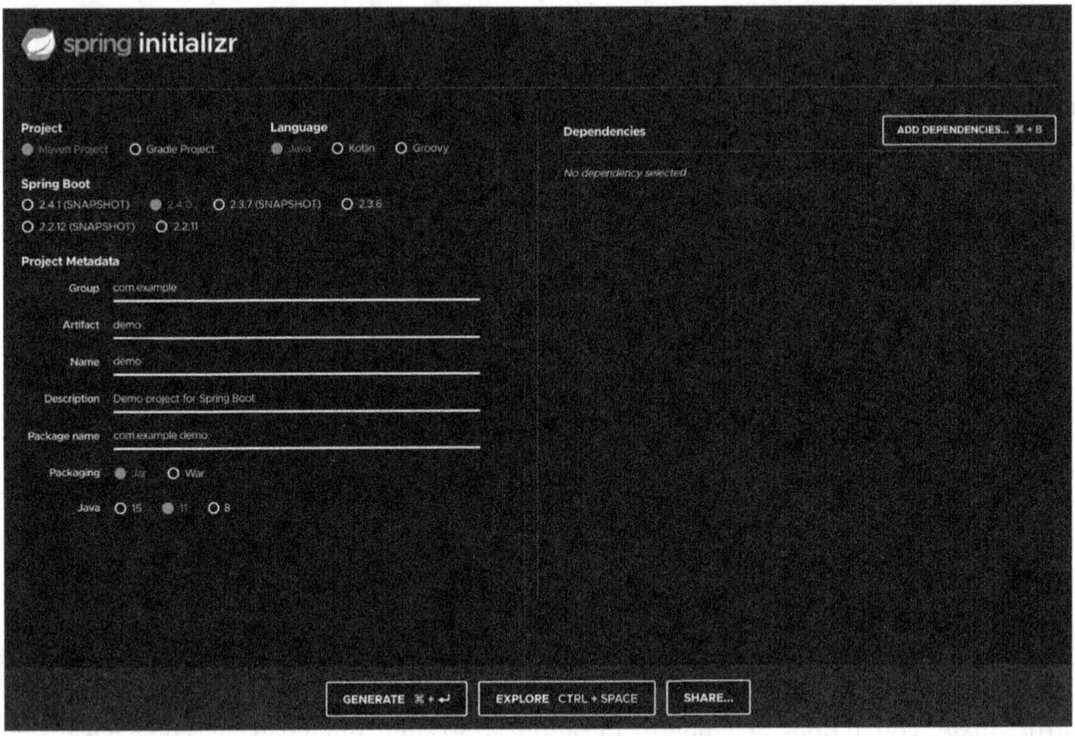

***Figure 16-3.*** *The Spring Initializr web page*

# Project Configuration

On the left side of the Spring Initializr page, you will see a variety of options for configuring a new Spring Boot application.

Start by selecting a project setting of Maven Project as you'll be using Apache Maven and the Maven client for build management of the application.

Next, select Java as the language and feel free to leave the default Spring Boot version as is. At the time I wrote this book, the default version was 2.4.0.

Figure 16-4 provides an example of what I've used for the project metadata settings, but feel free to customize depending on your needs and preferences.

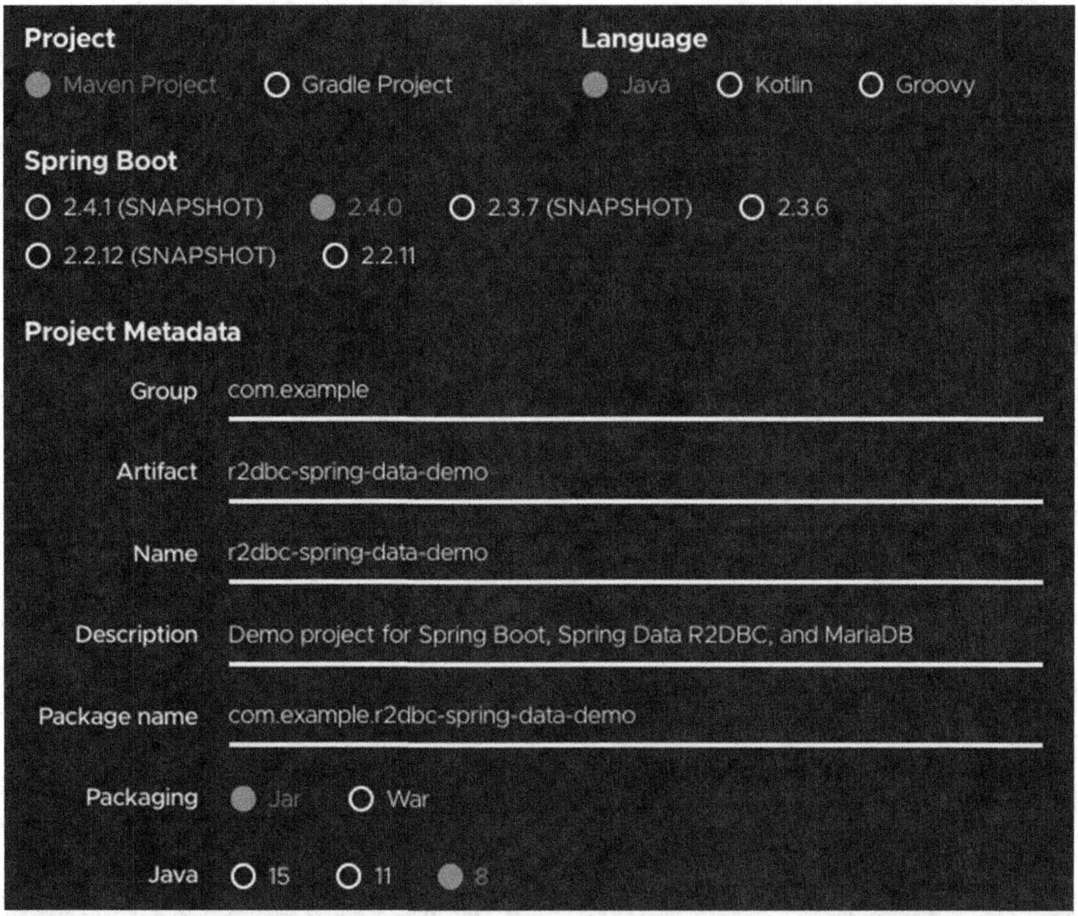

**Figure 16-4.** *Providing project settings for a new Spring Initializr generated application*

## Adding Dependencies

On the right of the Spring Initializr page is a section called "Dependencies," which can be used to add the Maven artifacts to the project that is to be generated. For the sample project, you'll need four dependencies indicated in Table 16-1.

***Table 16-1.*** *Names and descriptions of the Maven artifacts used within the sample project*

| Artifact Name | Description |
| --- | --- |
| MariaDB Driver | The MariaDB R2DBC driver artifact. |
| Spring Data R2DBC | The Spring Data R2DBC client library artifact. |
| Spring Reactive Web | A reactive framework library for web applications. |
| Lombok | A Java annotation library that helps reduce boilerplate code, that is, getter and setter methods for model objects. |

Click the "ADD DEPENDENCIES" button to prompt the workflow for searching for and adding dependencies to the project that is to be generated.

When the dependencies have been successfully added, you should see them populated on the page similar to Figure 16-5.

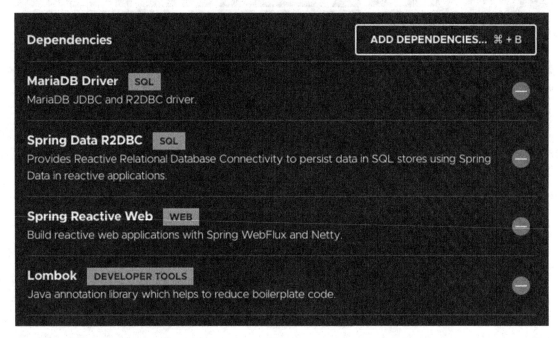

***Figure 16-5.*** *Dependencies that have been added to a new Spring Initializr–generated project*

# Generate a New Project

Finally, after the project settings have been provided and the dependencies added, you can generate a new Spring Boot application by clicking the "GENERATE" button at the bottom of the page.

Doing so will automatically download a compressed file, containing the project, to the default downloads location on your system.

After you've unpacked the file, you can use a code editor, or IDE, of your choice to open the project and inspect the files. As I pointed out earlier, Spring Initializr helps to reduce the amount of time spent constructing projects, including piecing together dependency hierarchies.

If you're curious as to what I mean by this, open and inspect the *pom.xml* file located within the top level of the *r2dbc-spring-data-demo* folder. In the pom.xml file, you'll notice a plethora of information about the project, including a dependencies section (Listing 16-1), which includes the dependencies you added using the Spring Initializr web interface.

***Listing 16-1.*** The dependencies for the Spring Initializr–generated project

```
<dependencies>
    <dependency>
        <groupId>org.springframework.boot</groupId>
        <artifactId>spring-boot-starter-data-r2dbc</artifactId>
    </dependency>
    <dependency>
        <groupId>org.springframework.boot</groupId>
        <artifactId>spring-boot-starter-webflux</artifactId>
    </dependency>
    <dependency>
        <groupId>org.mariadb</groupId>
        <artifactId>r2dbc-mariadb</artifactId>
        <version>0.8.4-rc</version>
    </dependency>
```

```
    <dependency>
        <groupId>org.projectlombok</groupId>
        <artifactId>lombok</artifactId>
        <optional>true</optional>
    </dependency>
    <dependency>
        <groupId>org.springframework.boot</groupId>
        <artifactId>spring-boot-starter-test</artifactId>
        <scope>test</scope>
    </dependency>
    <dependency>
        <groupId>io.projectreactor</groupId>
        <artifactId>reactor-test</artifactId>
        <scope>test</scope>
    </dependency>
</dependencies>
```

# Configuring Connections

In previous chapters, I've explained how connections to an underlying data source can be configured using an R2DBC driver directly. Ultimately the driver's code is responsible for handling all of the communication with the target data source, but part of the Spring Data R2DBC client's role is to help manage the connection workflow.

You can configure Spring Data R2DBC to use a specific driver and a connection to a target database by adding information to a single file called application.properties.

---

**Tip**    Spring Boot properties files are used to keep N number of properties in a single file to run the application in a different environment. In Spring Boot, properties are kept in the application.properties file under the classpath.

---

To do this, navigate to *r2dbc-spring-data-demo/src/main/resources/application.properties* and the connection information detailed in Listing 16-2.

***Listing 16-2.*** Spring Data R2DBC connection settings in the application. properties file

```
spring.r2dbc.url=r2dbc:mariadb://127.0.0.1:3306/todo
spring.r2dbc.username=app_user
spring.r2dbc.password=Password123!
```

---

**Tip**   For more information on Spring Data R2DBC configuration settings, including how to set up connection pooling, be sure to check out the official reference documentation at `https://docs.spring.io/spring-data/r2dbc/docs/ current/reference/html/#reference`.

---

# Spring Data Repositories

As I mentioned toward the beginning of this chapter, one of the goals of Spring Data repository abstraction is to help reduce the amount of boilerplate code required to implement data access layers for various persistence stores.

---

**Note**   In computer science, persistence is a noun describing data that outlives the process that created it.

---

In Spring, persistence can be handled through the use of a Data Access Object (DAO) layer. In such a case, the Spring DAO layer, as seen in Figure 16-6, is meant to function as a persistence manager, so the same application data access API would be given no matter if JDBC, R2DBC, JPA, or a native API were used.

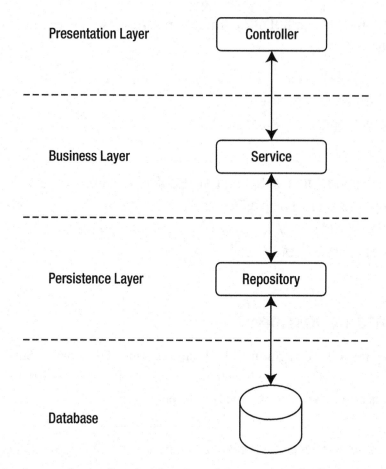

**Figure 16-6.** *A sample application layer architecture, including a persistence layer*

## Mapping Entities

Spring Data R2DBC entities are plain old Java objects (POJOs) and using Spring Data annotations can be mapped to relational database tables.

Using the @Table annotation, Spring Data R2DBC establishes a mapping between the Task class and the tasks table within your MariaDB *todo* database (Listing 16-3).

**Listing 16-3.** A Spring Data R2DBC mapped entity object

```
@Data
@RequiredArgsConstructor
@Table("tasks")
```

```
class Task {
    @Id
    private Integer id;
    @NonNull
    private String description;
    private Boolean completed;
}
```

**Tip**   The @Data annotation used in Listing 16-3 is an annotation available from the *Lombok* library and helps to eliminate the need to add *getter* and *setter* methods to the Task class. For more information about Project Lombok, be sure to check out https://projectlombok.org/.

## Creating a New Repository

Next, you can take advantage of a Spring Data R2DBC interface called ReactiveCrudRepository which provides generic CRUD operations on a repository for a specific type.

To use ReactiveCrudRepository, create a new interface named TasksRepository that extends ReactiveCrudRepository and supplies both a target entity type of Task and the primary key type of Integer (Listing 16-4).

***Listing 16-4.*** Creating a new repository implementation

```
interface TasksRepository extends ReactiveCrudRepository<Task, Integer> {
}
```

ReactiveCrudRepository follows reactive paradigms and uses Project Reactor types which are built on top of Reactive Streams. Basically, get ready to handle some Publisher objects.

## Querying Data

TasksRepository implements ReactiveCrudRepository, which provides several CRUD methods that can be used to interact with the *tasks* table within the *todo* database.

For instance, in Listings 16-5, 16-6, and 16-7, you can see a few of the CRUD method options available, where `tasksRepository` is an instantiated `TasksRepository` object.

***Listing 16-5.*** Select all records from the tasks table using the findAll method

```
Flux<Task> tasksPublisher = tasksRepository.findAll();
```

***Listing 16-6.*** Select a single task record by providing a primary key value to the findById method

```
Mono<Task> taskPublisher = tasksRepository.findById(1);
```

***Listing 16-7.*** Create a new task record

```
Task task = new Task("New Task");
Mono<Task> saveTaskPublisher = tasksRepository.save(task);
```

Keep in mind that Listings 16-5, 16-6, and 16-7 are only a few of the CRUD operations made available through `ReactiveCrudRepository`. For more information on `ReactiveCrudRepository`, please review the official documentation.

## Using Custom Queries

You also have the ability to add customized methods to a repository by adding method signatures to the repository interface (Listing 16-8).

***Listing 16-8.*** Custom defined query

```
interface TasksRepository extends ReactiveCrudRepository<Task, Integer> {
    @Modifying
    @Query("UPDATE tasks SET completed = :completed WHERE id = :id")
    Mono<Integer> updateStatus(Integer id, Boolean completed);
}
```

---

**Note**   The @Modifying annotation indicates that a query method should be considered a modifying query as that changes the way it needs to be executed. It is also required by Spring Data R2DBC repositories for all Data Manipulation Language (DML) and Data Definition Language (DDL) queries.

---

## Parameterization

In Chapters 6 and 13, you learned about the concept of parameterization within R2DBC and how placeholder values can be used to dynamically provide information to SQL statements.

Taking a closer look at the method added to the TasksRepository sample in Listing 16-8, Listing 16-9 focuses on the input parameters for the updateStatus method and how they can be used as parameters within the custom query specified through the use of the @Query annotation.

***Listing 16-9.*** Querying with parameters

```
@Query("UPDATE tasks SET completed = :completed WHERE id = :id")
Mono<Integer> updateStatus(Integer id, Boolean completed);
```

# Bringing It All Together

Now that you've learned how to properly configure the connection information using Spring Framework, examined how a mapping between the Task class and the underlying tasks table can be set up, and, finally, gotten an idea of what it's like to use a custom implementation of ReactiveCrudRepository to handle persistence, you now have the foundation allowing you to read and write information from and to your MariaDB database using R2DBC!

In Listing 16-10, I've brought everything together in one, cohesive sample that you use to replace all of the contents in */r2dbc-spring-data-demo/src/main/java/com/example/r2dbcspringdatademo/R2dbcSpringDataDemoApplication.java*.

***Listing 16-10.*** The complete code sample for R2dbcSpringDataDemoApplication.java

```
package com.example.r2dbcspringdatademo;

import org.springframework.beans.factory.annotation.Autowired;
import org.springframework.boot.SpringApplication;
import org.springframework.boot.autoconfigure.SpringBootApplication;
import org.springframework.data.annotation.Id;
import org.springframework.data.r2dbc.repository.Modifying;
import org.springframework.data.r2dbc.repository.Query;
```

```
import org.springframework.data.r2dbc.repository.config.
EnableR2dbcRepositories;
import org.springframework.data.relational.core.mapping.Table;
import org.springframework.data.repository.reactive.ReactiveCrudRepository;
import org.springframework.http.HttpStatus;
import org.springframework.http.ResponseEntity;
import org.springframework.stereotype.Service;
import org.springframework.transaction.annotation.Transactional;
import org.springframework.web.bind.annotation.DeleteMapping;
import org.springframework.web.bind.annotation.GetMapping;
import org.springframework.web.bind.annotation.PostMapping;
import org.springframework.web.bind.annotation.PutMapping;
import org.springframework.web.bind.annotation.RequestBody;
import org.springframework.web.bind.annotation.RequestMapping;
import org.springframework.web.bind.annotation.RequestParam;
import org.springframework.web.bind.annotation.RestController;

import lombok.Data;
import lombok.NonNull;
import lombok.RequiredArgsConstructor;
import reactor.core.publisher.Flux;
import reactor.core.publisher.Mono;

@SpringBootApplication
@EnableR2dbcRepositories
public class R2dbcSpringDataDemoApplication {

    public static void main(String[] args) {
        SpringApplication.run(R2dbcSpringDataDemoApplication.class, args);
    }

}

@RestController
@RequestMapping("/tasks")
class TasksController {

    @Autowired
    private TaskService service;
```

```
@GetMapping()
public ResponseEntity<Flux<Task>> get() {
    return ResponseEntity.ok(this.service.getAllTasks());
}

@PostMapping()
public ResponseEntity<Mono<Task>> post(@RequestBody Task task) {
    if (service.isValid(task)) {
        return ResponseEntity.ok(this.service.createTask(task));
    }
    return ResponseEntity.status(HttpStatus.I_AM_A_TEAPOT).build();
}

@PutMapping()
public ResponseEntity<Mono<Task>> put(@RequestBody Task task) {
    if (service.isValid(task)) {
        return ResponseEntity.ok(this.service.updateTask(task));
    }
    return ResponseEntity.status(HttpStatus.I_AM_A_TEAPOT).build();
}

@PutMapping("/updatestatus")
public ResponseEntity<Mono<Integer>> updateStatus(@RequestParam int id,
@RequestParam Boolean completed) {
    if (id > 0) {
        return ResponseEntity.ok(this.service.updateTaskStatusById(id,
        completed));
    }
    return ResponseEntity.status(HttpStatus.I_AM_A_TEAPOT).build();
}

@DeleteMapping()
public ResponseEntity<Mono<Void>> delete(@RequestParam int id) {
    if (id > 0) {
        return ResponseEntity.ok(this.service.deleteTask(id));
    }
```

```java
            return ResponseEntity.status(HttpStatus.I_AM_A_TEAPOT).build();
    }
}

@Service
class TaskService {

    @Autowired
    private TasksRepository repository;

    public Boolean isValid(final Task task) {
        if (task != null && !task.getDescription().isEmpty()) {
            return true;
        }
        return false;
    }

    public Flux<Task> getAllTasks() {
        return this.repository.findAll();
    }

    public Mono<Task> createTask(final Task task) {
        return this.repository.save(task);
    }

    @Transactional
    public Mono<Task> updateTask(final Task task) {

        return this.repository.findById(task.getId())
                .flatMap(t -> {
                    t.setDescription(task.getDescription());
                    t.setCompleted(task.getCompleted());
                    return this.repository.save(t);
                });
    }
```

```java
    public Mono<Integer> updateTaskStatusById(Integer id, Boolean
    completed) {
        return this.repository.updateStatus(id, completed);
    }

    @Transactional
    public Mono<Void> deleteTask(final int id){
        return this.repository.findById(id)
                .flatMap(this.repository::delete);
    }
}

interface TasksRepository extends ReactiveCrudRepository<Task, Integer> {
    @Modifying
    @Query("UPDATE tasks SET completed = :completed WHERE id = :id")
    Mono<Integer> updateStatus(Integer id, Boolean completed);
}

@Data
@RequiredArgsConstructor
@Table("tasks")
class Task {
    @Id
    private Integer id;
    @NonNull
    private String description;
    private Boolean completed;
}
```

In combination with setting the application.properties configuration necessary and the persistence implementation you've learned about in this chapter, Listing 16-10 also includes two additional classes: TaskService and TaskController.

Using libraries made available through the Spring Web Reactive library, previously added as a dependency, the TaskController class exposes API endpoints.

Using Inversion of Control (IoC), provided by Spring Framework, the TaskController class creates and uses a TaskService object as an intermediary, business-level mechanism to interact with TasksRepository.

---

**Note**   In software engineering, Inversion of Control (IoC) is a programming principle. IoC inverts the flow of control as compared to traditional control flow. In IoC, custom-written portions of a computer program receive the flow of control from a generic framework.

---

# Testing It Out

Having put all the pieces together, it's time to check out the running application to see the fruits of your labor. You'll start by building and running the application. From there you'll be able to make HTTP requests to the endpoints that have been exposed using `TaskController`.

## Build and Run the Project

While you're more than welcome to use whatever build process or tool, such as an IDE like Eclipse, that you're comfortable with to build and run the application, you can also use the Apache Maven client like we've done in previous chapters.

Upon opening a new terminal window and navigating to the root location of the *r2dbc-spring-data-demo* project, you can execute the command in Listing 16-11 to build the Spring Boot application using Maven.

***Listing 16-11.*** Build the application using the Apache Maven client

```
mvn package
```

Once you've successfully built the application, you can use the command in Listing 16-12 to run the application.

***Listing 16-12.*** Run the application using the Apache Maven client

```
mvn spring-boot:run
```

# Call an Endpoint

Finally, to bring this chapter's coding exercise to a conclusion, and now that you've successfully built and run the application, it's time to call the endpoints you've exposed through the `TaskController` class.

There are many options available for making HTTP requests. For the purposes of the following sample, I've opted to use curl, which is a command-line tool for sending and retrieving data using URL syntax. You can find more information on curl support as well as how to download the client at `https://curl.se/`.

Using curl, as indicated in Listing 16-13, you can execute a GET request to retrieve all of the tasks in your MariaDB *todo.tasks* table.

***Listing 16-13.*** Call the tasks endpoint to retrieve all the records in the MariaDB todo.tasks table

```
curl http://localhost:8080/tasks
```

# Show Me the Code

You can find a complete, fully compilable sample application in the GitHub repository dedicated to this book. If you haven't already done so, simply navigate to `https://github.com/apress/r2dbc-revealed` to either `git clone` or directly download the contents of the repository. From there you can find a sample application dedicated to this chapter in the *ch16* folder.

# Summary

There's no question that using an R2DBC significantly cuts down on the amount of development time and effort spent constructing a reusable data access workflow. In this chapter, you learned about Spring Framework, Spring Boot, and how Spring Data helps to abstract away a large amount of the complexity that exists within a data persistence layer. Building on those fundamentals, you also gained an understanding of the Spring Data R2DBC client library and how it can use an R2DBC driver to create fully reactive applications.

# Index

## A

ACID properties, 56
Apache Maven
    dependencies, 123
    project, building, 124
    project structure, 123
    SCM command, 123
Application layer architecture, 196
Application programming
    interface (API), 17, 186
application.properties, 194
Asynchronous Database
    Access (ADBA), 19
Asynchronous data streams
    back pressure, 15, 16
    data stream, 13, 14
Atomicity, 55
Auto-commit mode, 58, 59
Auto-generated values, 72

## B

Back pressure, 15, 16, 24
Batching statements, 70, 155
beginTransaction method, 59, 163
BiFunction, 150
Binary large objects (BLOBs), 95
Binary types, 93
Binding parameters, 70, 154

## B

Blob factory method, 96
block method, 133
Boolean data type, 92

## C

Categorize exceptions
    non-transient exceptions, 108
    transient exceptions, 109
Character large objects (CLOBs), 96
Character types, 91
Client libraries, R2DBC
    client creation, 115
    existing client library, 116
Clob interface, 97
Closeable interface, 52
Closeable interfaces, 38, 39
Collection types, 95
Column metadata
    interface, 84
    optional methods, 85–87
    required methods, 85
ColumnMetadata interface, 84
Connection
    closing, 134
    interface, 162
    validating, 134
ConnectionFactories
    discovery, 47
    R2DBC URL, 48

207

Printed in the United States
by Baker & Taylor Publisher Services